When the
CROWD STOPS ROARING

The inspirational memoir
of an extraordinary All Black

Neven MacEwan

WSP
WILD SIDE PUBLISHING
real stories. real hope.

wildsidepublishing.com

When the
CROWD STOPS ROARING

The inspirational memoir
of an extraordinary All Black

Neven MacEwan

wildsidepublishing.com

Wild Side Publishing
PO Box 33, Ruawai 0549
Northland, New Zealand
wildsidepublishing.com

Copyright ©2019 Neven MacEwan
nevenmacewan.com

All rights reserved. No part of this publication may be reproduced, distributed, or transmitted in any form or by any means, including photocopying, recording, or other electronic or mechanical methods, without the prior written permission of the publisher, except with brief quotations embodied in reviews and certain other non-commercial uses permitted by copyright law.

Cover design and book layout by Janet Curle wildsidepublishing.com
Proofreading and light copy editing by Sue Beguely triplecoilscript.co.nz
All Black team photos supplied courtesy of New Zealand Rugby Museum Inc.

Cataloguing in Publication Data:
Title: When the Crowd Stops Roaring
ISBN: 978-0-473-46883-5 (pbk)
ISBN: 978-0-473-46884-2 (epub)

Subjects: Memoir, Autobiography, New Zealand Non-Fiction, All Blacks, Rugby, Sport, Chaplaincy, Alcoholism, Recovery, Testimony

First printing 2019 benefitz.co.nz
International listing 2019 ingramspark.com

Dedication

This book is dedicated to my amazing and very talented wife Jeannette, our family—Doug, Bruce, Angus and Jeannie. Please accept my appreciation and love for being the greatest supporters one could wish for when things couldn't get any worse. I thank each of you for the important part you played.

Contents

	Foreword: Keith Quinn	ix
	Prologue	xiii
1	In the Beginning	1
2	Part I: The Boy Beautiful	9
	Part II: Raising Richmond	18
	Part III: My Mother's Son	21
	Part IV: Rise of the Gentle Giant	28
3	My School Teacher Career	37
4	Rugby Tests and Jerseys	49
5	Travel Experiences and Work	75
	Photo Gallery	99
6	The Tale of the Jerseys Concludes	115
7	Spiritual Awakening	125
A	Appendix: CV & Personal Statement	187
B	Appendix: More About Rooney & Correspondence	191
C	Appendix: Match Details	197
	Acknowledgements	201

NEVEN MACEWAN

Foreword

I was a skinny kid in 1954 when our family moved to Wellington. We lived on the hillside slopes behind Athletic Park. It was the perfect location for us country kids to be raised. We were at Athletic Park for every rugby game we could get to. As there was never any charge to get in, the Park became our second home. And for me its closeness to home greatly influenced what was to follow in my adult life.

I became saturated with rugby. I loved the All Blacks; I loved the Wellington representative team (especially when they trained on Sunday mornings—the perfect place to go to instead of church!) and I loved the battles between all the different local clubs.

Athletic wore blue and black hoops. They had many a dasher in the backs. I remember John MacGibbon the handsome, loping winger who lived around the road from us. Jim Johnstone was a stylish fullback. Rod Heeps and Russell Watt became worthy All Blacks and we thought the halfback Barry Cull might well have become one. Taniru Kite was hooker for the Maori All Blacks. There were many other fine players and in those days, of course, Athletic had the thundering lock forwards Dave Harker and Neven MacEwan.

I have known the last-named for a number of years now. I have never told Nev this before but, as a kid, I paid him the highest compliment a kid could. I kept clippings about him. I didn't do it for every club player just the ones who were my favourites. MacEwan was one and I still have many of the clippings.

NEVEN MACEWAN

For a start he was so big! He towered over most of his teammates and opponents and as each game and season unfolded he expanded his talent into that of a true international rugby player. I loved the way MacEwan of Athletic, Wellington and New Zealand could leap at line-out time. From a standing upwards jump, and completely unassisted, Nev's feet seemed to rise above the earth's crust! He was a great line-out jumper. Better, I dare to suggest, than any All Black leaper of recent times.

I saw Nev play his best rugby in the late fifties and early sixties. There were few players who could match him from any team of the many who came to Wellington, be they representative or touring teams. He was a top All Black in his time reaching 20 tests at a time when there were only four or five tests a year. It should be remembered that he played for his country over seven long seasons—no mean feat. He might have done more but for persistent knee injuries.

His loyalty to Wellington was memorable too. He passed Don McIntosh's record of most games for Wellington in 1966 when he was in his twelfth season in first class rugby.

Several other things I remember about Nev's rugby. He organised the ground-breaking world tour for his Athletic club team in 1966. That team's feats were truly of epic proportions. There were twelve games in five countries with only 25 players: a blockbuster tour unmatched by any club team since. As a young man I admired their courage and achievements. I have a faded picture of them on tour among my 40-year-old collection.

One other clipping from my study has caught my eye. It comes from The Dominion Post of 17 May 1967 and is headlined, 'Clash of Views Ousts MacEwan'. To me this story epitomises the fundamental commitment Nev gave to the game and his club, Athletic. The ousting referred to Nev declaring himself unavailable for any representative rugby games that year if they interfered with playing club rugby. The Wellington selector that year was the great Bill Freeman, also an Athletic stalwart. There was a standoff: Freeman wanted all players for his rep teams but MacEwan stood by his club. Surely modern All

Blacks would look at Nev's attitude and wonder if he was mad! But that was MacEwan, a rugby man of conviction and belief.

So has it been for Nev in his life away from rugby. We know of his work in recent years and his strong Christian devotion. In the decades since his active football days there have been tough times for Nev. He has not shied away from them in his story. I am glad he has written openly of his life's experiences. I admire him for that and commend this story to you for what it is, a life worth living. It is the story of a sportsman who has known the best and worst side of being a very public New Zealander, and of the club he has remained loyal to.

The skinny kid of all those years ago has also kept hundreds of rugby quotations. Do I have one which applies to and celebrates Nev MacEwan and this book? I think so. Rene Benesis, a Narbonne and French hooker of the 1960s, said on his retirement from the game,

> In life there were sometimes narrow doors for me, but rugby eventually widened my horizons. I am deeply indebted to the game. I always tried to repay my debt. I hope I did it in a lifetime of 80-minute installments.

Keith Quinn
Broadcaster & Sports Commentator
Wellington

NEVEN MACEWAN

Prologue

In June 1979, while I was working in the family book and toy shop in Palmerston North, a detective walked into the store and asked me to call into the police station as soon as possible. I immediately knew something was not right, but what I did not know was how serious it was.

I went in later in the day and was ushered into an interview room where I was asked questions about the accounting books pertaining to the National Travel Association (Manawatu Branch) Inc. They were interested in three entries and wanted to know where the money had gone. I confessed I needed the funds at the time to meet personal commitments and the money had been returned at a later date.

I agreed I had no authorisation to make the payments and I was subsequently charged with theft as a servant and discharged on bail to appear in court the following Monday. When they had fingerprinted me, the enormity of it all started to hit home. These ink-stained fingers were part of a pair of hands which time and time again had reached high above the opposition to take the ball in the line-outs, accompanied by the cheers of the roaring crowd. Now they were being branded criminal for life.

I walked away from the police station in total confusion believing this nightmare would go away and I would soon wake up. I went home and pretended everything was all right; I told no one, not even my wife Jeannette or lawyer. I felt alone and ashamed; I had no one to turn for help, so I did what I knew best to solve my problems. I hit the bottle in a big way until I was out of it and went to sleep in drunken oblivion.

I woke up the next day and went to work at the shop at the usual time and worked as if nothing had happened. This routine carried on for the rest of the week, but I began to realise the court appearance was never going to go away. I vividly remember the Saturday 48 hours before my appearance in front of the judge on Monday. I delivered the magazines to our subagents around Terrace End and went back to the shop for a short while. I went home for lunch, did a couple of jobs and then went back to the shop on the pretense I had some paperwork to finish. I sat there at the desk agitated about what I was going to do.

There was nothing I could do; hence, I had to get out of this mess 'my way'. The only way out was to eliminate the problem. The problem was me. It was at this moment I decided to take my own life. This would be the ultimate selfish act, thinking only of myself and not the aftermath others would have to face and clean up. All of this turmoil in my life was the result of wrong choices I'd made over a period of 30 years.

I won't discuss precisely what I did, but clearly my attempts were a failure, and the next few hours remained a living hell. How had I got into such a mess? What did I do to get out of it? Where did my most prized rugby jerseys go, and why did my life's journey lead me to Wales and a reconnection with my achievements as an All Black?

For answers to these questions, let us turn back the clock and journey together through my story of hope.

1. In the beginning

> "When one door closes another one opens.
> What you believe is the worst moment of your life could
> turn out to be the beginning of a new and better life."
> ~Margie Tsoukias

> "You just have to work through your bad races,
> so you can look forward to the good ones."
> ~Hamish Carter

THE MACEWAN CLAN

It's interesting how life and family have a habit of coming full circle. I was born in Auckland, and spent my childhood in Nelson. My All Black and rugby-playing years were spent in Wellington.

But my links to Manawatu and its neighbours were formed before I was born. Mum and Dad met on board RMS Rangitiki and lived in Palmerston North at picturesque 1 Elmira Avenue from 1930 to 1933. My older brother Bill was born there on 18 February 1931, and my father made the first night flight between Marton and Palmerston North in a Tiger Moth. If you continue reading you will see that the most important years of my life and those of my family were spent in Palmerston North.

However, there's a lot of water to tread before we get back to Palmy. Or should I say milk?

Much ado About Milking

On my paternal side I am a second generation New Zealander, the third son of Ian Arthur and Ivy Heather MacEwan, and grandson of James Ballantyne and Mary Elizabeth MacEwan. The far-off lands of Canada and Scotland are most prominent in my ancestry. But let us begin with my grandfather, James Ballantyne MacEwan. He was born in Stratford, Ontario in 1866. 'JB' (as he was called) arrived in New Zealand from Canada in 1894. He served in the Canadian Department of Agriculture where he had helped establish farm training schools. JB was then brought out to New Zealand by the Ministry of Agriculture to help develop our fledgling dairy industry. He established two dairy training schools, one in Stratford and the other in Edendale. Over the following decades these educational facilities would produce many of New Zealand's dairy farmers who would bring in valuable income from butter exports. He became the Dairy Commissioner, but he wasn't just a fancy foreign bureaucrat by any means.

During his two years in the job he made some rather useful contacts and, as we shall see, had some big ideas. At 28 years of age he decided to go into business and in the period 1896–1902, JB did a number of things. He:

- Brought his two brothers George and Arthur MacEwan from Canada
- Married Mary Fisher, the daughter of MP for Wellington Central, FMB Fisher (1905–1914), in 1900
- Bought some fancy butter- and cheese-packing machinery back in Canada and shipped it to New Zealand
- Moved to Dunedin where he established JB MacEwan & Co Ltd., later moving the company to Wellington

By 1902, the company became the sole supplier in New Zealand of the Lawrence and Kennedy Milking Apparatus which had been invented in Scotland. It was the first commercially available suction-based milking machine ever produced. The speed of acquisition shows just how forward-thinking JB and his brothers were as the machine was literally hot off the press.

It would eventually make a huge impact on our farming but, in its infancy, the machine wasn't perfect. Therefore, JB made a few Kiwi-based modifications. He then had to prove the legitimacy of the invention to numerous doubters. This he did and JB was set to become one of the most influential and knowledgeable businessmen in New Zealand. Indeed, there is one story about JB's knowledge of milk production and incredible skill in taste-testing dairy products which cemented his place as the leading authority of dairy in the world.

He was once invited to judge the butter competition at the annual Taranaki A&P show. All entries were meticulously tasted by JB who had to select the three finalists. However, JB hit something of a snag; he approached the organising committee and told them (I am sorry for the terrible pun which follows) he couldn't 'separate' the first two placings and had to declare a tie for first.

The committee objected as it was unheard of to share the prize. Would he mind trying again and declaring a sole winner. Understanding the predicament the committee was in he evaluated both entries again. He came back and declared his original judgement still stood. After the announcement was made there was a lot of heated debate and many probably believed JB to be an arrogant spoiler. That is until the two winning entrants announced their butters had come out of the same churn. This revelation left the organisers in awe of JB, whose rather large ego greatly appreciated the admiration.

Thus, few dairy farms in the country are untouched by JB in some shape or form and the company lives on in New Zealand as MacEwan Machinery Ltd.

The Kerr Family

My mother's father was William John Kerr; he was born in Lossiemouth, Moray, Scotland on 20 July 1877. William became a successful jute/hessian merchant in Dundee until the decline of the industry in the mid-1920s. He'd married a Glaswegian by the name of Elizabeth Barclay whom we knew as Granny Kerr; she was born 19 February 1878. They lived in Carnoustie until the family moved to New Zealand in 1929. Granny Kerr's father had been a lighthouse keeper on one of Thomas Edison's lighthouses, and it seems the Barclays, who'd settled in North East Scotland, were decidedly trans-Atlantic. They had played a role in the American War of Independence, were Quakers, and involved themselves in shipping and trade. William and Elizabeth had two children: my Uncle Neven born in 1904, and my mother Ivy Heather who appeared on 28 July 1905.

The males of the family weren't blessed with the longevity of the females. Grandad Kerr died aged 62 in Auckland in 1940, so I never really had the chance to know him. Neven, whom I would get to know only marginally better (for reasons you shall find out later on), died in Auckland aged 56. Granny Kerr died in Wellington in 1965 aged 86.

As a result of her long life she witnessed my rugby career from beginning to end. She was there for all of us boys in our sporting endeavours, but I formed an especially close relationship with her which was something I treasured because she didn't suffer those she considered fools for long. When I started playing rugby in 1949 she was my greatest fan and loyal supporter right up until her death. When I played home games for the first fifteen at Nelson College in 1951–52, Granny Kerr would arrive at midday no matter what the weather. She would sit on the seats at the top of the terrace on half way and wait for the 3.00 pm kick-off. You could set your clock by when she arrived.

Mum's life was an interesting one. In 1921 she received notification from Oxford and Cambridge Schools Examination Board that she had satisfied the examiners in the subjects of Arithmetic, English, History and Geography in the Lower Certificate Examinations. These were like high school University Entrance exams here in New Zealand but, with today's qualification system, I don't rightly know the equivalent qualification. Needless to say Mum was clearly bright and would have made an excellent academic. When she was 21 years old she almost died in a nasty car crash in her home town of Carnoustie. The quick actions of a bystander saved Mum's life, but she did spend a long time in intensive care. It's hard to say if the injuries she sustained affected her in the long term.

As part of her recovery, Grandad Kerr took the family around the world sailing on the New Zealand Shipping Company's liner RMS *Rangitiki*. The *Rangitiki* sailed from Wellington on 10 May 1929 and arrived at Southampton 14 June 1929, travelling via Pitcairn Island and the Panama Canal. On board were three families all travelling First Saloon: Mr and Mrs JB MacEwan and son Ian; Mr and Mrs WJ Kerr with their son Neven and daughter Ivy Heather; and Mr and Mrs V Barker and their two daughters Miss EM and Miss JM (Joy).

It was on this voyage where Dad met Mum and Neven Kerr met Joy Barker. Both couples would marry the following year in New Zealand. Unfortunately, it wasn't all happy-ever-after stuff for the Kerr family. Within a few years of this journey my grandfather, William John Kerr, lost his business in Scotland when India stopped exporting jute. As a result he and Granny Kerr decided to move closer to their daughter and settled in Auckland in 1938.

DEEPER ISSUES
Mum's convalescence from the accident was a long one, both physically and psychologically. Her initial debt to Dad was great, so great, she was to say years later in spite of everything, 'If there hadn't been an Ian, there wouldn't have been a Heather.' There certainly wouldn't have been me either.

Dad's natural charisma, and charm had given her the motivation to carry on at an extremely difficult time in her life. Nevertheless, this would be a fleeting triumph. Medical treatments, medications and psychiatric support weren't like they are today. On top of possible ongoing medical complications for a head injury, her family and her husband's dramatic reversals of fortune would have been horrible. Hence, I think my mother raised us while struggling from what we would term Post Traumatic Stress Disorder (PTSD) today.

Fortunately, Granny Kerr and my mother were very close. Nevertheless, while the bond they shared kept my mother going after Dad's decline, it also, sadly, locked these two outwardly tough, but vulnerable women into their own world. They could be quite negative and judgemental towards those outside of their control. It is important for the reader to understand how I was brought up, the struggles Mum presented me with, but also to have empathy for these two women.

Despite their challenges, I now prefer to remember them for the incredibly capable, tough and smart survivors they both were. Mum was fond of bold statements, and she certainly lived by them. For example, consider the statement she gave to an interviewer:

> We were brought up to have the courage of our convictions. After all, all we have to answer for is our own life. It might inconvenience other people, but my credentials are a life lived – good, bad or indifferent. You don't get all good credentials.

The tone of defiance is so completely Scottish; you can see how they've given the English nightmares for centuries.

High Society

When my mother was married in Wellington in 1930, there were 19 members in the bridal party and 400 guests. Of these guests, Mum personally knew only 25. They also had a photographer and, as Ian was a 16 mm enthusiast, they brought along a film-maker. While it may be commonplace today for a wedding to include photographers and a digital camera operator, the 1930s' equivalents were extremely rare and expensive.

Hence, there is a film of the MacEwan-Kerr wedding. The film, entitled *Wedding Bells: 400 Guests at MacEwan-Kerr Wedding, 1930*, includes footage of many of the politicians of the time. It is now part of the collection of Ngā Taonga Sound and Vision (formerly the National Film Archive).[1] The wedding took place on 10 April 1930 at Old St Paul's. The synopsis of the film in the National Film Archive makes it clear that a fixed camera was set up outside the church showing scenes of the wedding party and guests entering and later leaving after the ceremony. The wedding also made it into the national weekly pictorial magazine called *The New Zealand Freelance* for 16 April 1930.

The reception was held at the MacEwan home in Fitzherbert Terrace, Wellington. As Mum recalled,

> It was built so that no earthquake could shake it—double brick, with steel up the middle. When they took it down for the motorway, they had awful trouble.

However, before it was destroyed in the mid-1960s, it had passed through a period of ownership by the US Government which had bought it from the Estate of JB MacEwan. It was used as the official US embassy in the years up to its demise. The foundations were solid, the structure was sound, and I remember it as a lovely home when I stayed with my grandparents in 1939 just before the outbreak of World War II.

In Control and Out of Touch

After their marriage, Dad was appointed manager of the Palmerston North branch of JB MacEwan and Co. in Rangitikei Street and resided at 1 Elmira Avenue. Mum's accident had thrown her child-bearing ability in doubt. Hence, when she gave birth to the first of her four sons, Bill, she was greatly relieved. As a result their time in Palmerston North was probably the happiest Mum and Dad had as a couple before the true extent of Dad's alcoholism became a problem.

Dad faced major problems working for the autocratic and, by now, rather haughty JB MacEwan. Dad's prospects in the family firm were

---
[1] The film reference number is F651. http://data.filmarchive.org.nz

secure and he showed great ability in his work, especially in terms of business sense. Dad thought differently from Grandad. JB could enhance anything he came across and, as we have seen, he could offer sage-like advice in his particular field of interest. He was brilliant in his functionality but no visionary although, thanks to everybody indulging his ego, he felt he was. This led to an overbearing arrogance when dealing with suggestions from his friends and family about potential ventures. So much so, he felt his creative and quite gifted son was nothing but a dreamer.

Dad had undertaken a classical education at Cambridge University in England, as was only fitting for a son of his father's rank. He did well, but apparently felt deeply restricted. My older brother Pat, recalled that what Dad had really wanted to be was a refrigeration engineer. This might not sound glamorous, but Dad had seen the money made in international refrigerated shipping for Kiwi beef farmers.

Now, back then no two ships were equipped with standardised refrigeration systems. It was an awfully hit and miss, seat-of-the-pants business. Dad saw ways in which the MacEwan company could create and supply parts for modern shipping refrigeration units. However, he saw another big opportunity to make money in the domestic refrigeration market.

So when he returned from a business trip to the US, which had become the refrigeration hub of the world, he met up with JB and boldly announced that field refrigeration had become very promising. Moreover, he told JB that the enormous American company Frigidaire was interested in JB MacEwan & Co becoming its New Zealand agent. JB laughed and dismissed the proposal out of hand. Of course, the joke was on JB. The industry and the son he mocked would have seen him and his business become one of the richest and most influential engineering firms in the Southern Hemisphere.

2. Part I: The Boy Beautiful

My oldest brother James William, more commonly known as Bill, was born in Palmerston North on 18 February 1931. Soon after, Mum, Dad and Bill left Palmy when Dad was promoted to manage the Machinery Division of JB MacEwan & Co in Penrose, Auckland. They took up residence at 1 St Vincent Avenue, Remuera. Soon my older brother Pat (Hugh Patrick) was born there on 9 May 1932. The house witnessed another arrival two years later when I was born on the 1 May 1934.

My recollections of Remuera are a little vague. My family and I spent four years there before we moved to 4 Edmund Street, St Heliers in 1938. The move came at an awkward time for my family as JB had sent Dad to a specialist in Harley Street, London to help him overcome his alcohol problem.

During the four or five months Dad was away, we found we were neighbours of the Pritchard family. Our time with them was incredibly brief, but these amazing people left deep impressions on all of us. Rae Pritchard, her brother Stan and sister Noelene (Bud) were great people. The person chiefly responsible for their development was their mum, a blind woman by the name of Rosie Pritchard.

My mother and Granny Kerr could be very selective about who they would associate with. This meant they wouldn't go out of their way for just anyone. Yet there was something truly magnetic about Rosie, and a friendship blossomed …

> Your mother, and Granny Kerr taught my mother to cook. They would dictate recipes to Rosie who would write them down in Braille for later reference on a cumbersome wooden frame which had a two-line holed brass template which moved downwards as each succeeding line was punched into the paper with a stylus—very laborious, but a wonderful thing for them to have done.
>
> As a result of their input Rosie was able to do without the housekeepers she'd been relying on and who she felt were coming between her and us kids. Nev, their impact was enormous. I remember one recipe they taught her was a butter cake recipe which was varied by adding cocoa for a chocolate cake. Rosie had no problem producing the baked cakes, [but] icing them defeated her and that was left to Noelene who was ten years older than me and could therefore manage the manoeuvre with ease.[2]

Rosie was one of the leading advocates for the blind in Auckland at the time. Moreover, she also gave me my first nickname. Mum and Granny Kerr had called me 'beautiful'. Looking back, something must have happened on the way to the circus. However, when I went over to visit for the first time she ran her hands over my face and asked my name. I replied, 'Beautiful,' and from our very first meeting Beautiful became her name for me.

While the name was a source of amusement amongst the neighbours, I was much too young to be embarrassed or shamed by it. Sadly, in later years, I became paranoid about anyone finding out I was ever called Beautiful; it was not the image I wanted as a rugby player. When I hit rock bottom many years later I would reclaim that name. Indeed, a little Christian song, 'Something Beautiful,' is the story of my new life. My mind drifts back to Rosie whenever I hear it.

---

[2] Rae Curry, March 2018.

MY FAMILY OF MANY MOVES

When I was going through my old notes for this chapter, it struck me how difficult it would be to explain my movements around Nelson and my brief time in Wellington during the period 1939–1949.

In late 1939 we moved to Richmond (then a smaller satellite town of Nelson), to the orchard property 'Freshfields' on Hill Street. We attended Richmond Primary School from 1940–1943. During this time Michael, our youngest brother, was born on 5 October 1941. In 1944 we attended Wellesley College, Wellington for one year as boarders, and then back briefly to Richmond and a new home on Upper Queen Street. We then moved to 'Balgowan', Spring Grove, Nelson in 1946. From here I attended Wakefield School from 1947–1948 before going to Nelson College in 1949.

I grew a thicker skin while at Freshfields; I unconsciously developed a knack for turning a bad situation into a positive (a talent I lost as I descended into alcohol abuse as an adult). By nature my mother could be highly authoritarian. Punishment meant punishment, and she was good at it. However, I didn't learn until later that she had noted and quietly admired my innate optimism.

> You simply couldn't punish him, as a child. He turned every punishment into a diversion. He was told to polish a floor once, and turned the polishing pads into skates complete with two brothers in on the act. Another time, (I've forgotten what he'd done wrong), I told him to go and chop some wood. He went off, and I went about my work and I forgot about him. Hours later, I called the family in for tea, and there's no Nev.
>
> I said to the boys, 'Where is he?'
>
> 'Oh,' said Bill, 'he's out in the woodshed.'
>
> 'Go and call him in, would you? It's time he was here.'
>
> So Bill goes off, and he's gone for far too long before he comes back and reports, 'He says he'll be here soon.'

Well, I'm getting a bit annoyed by now. 'What do you mean, soon?' I say. 'It's time he was here!'

'Well, he's busy,' said Bill. 'He hasn't finished yet. Can we have our dinner now?'

By now, I'm becoming curious—he should have finished the job I gave him long before. So I take myself out to the woodshed to see for myself, and I can't even see him. He'd split up dozens of pieces of firewood, and built himself a great big castle, an elaborate thing, and he's totally engrossed over in the far corner finishing off the last battlement. I'm the one who ended up being punished as I was hungry. He'd simply got an afternoon's diversion out of it all and an artistic masterpiece to boot. I reminded him of it years later, in Palmerston North when things were so bad, how he'd turned every punishment into a pleasure, and he just said, 'I think I've forgotten the art.'[3]

Crime and Nourishment

In Auckland, a nanny assisted Mum in the care of the three of us. We'd lost her by the time we moved to Nelson. So Mum now became our primary caregiver. We would learn much later on that as small children we were a great source of comfort to her. Unfortunately, the comfort we gave her as preschoolers turned into a more complex range of emotions as we grew up.

Mum believed in a firm approach, and was not beyond smacking us if we did not meet the standards she had set. This was all well and good in an era where harsh discipline was the rite of passage for most kids. However, Mum brooked no quarter and everyone was punished in equal measure. But, this 'equal treatment' tended to fall hardest on me because I was the smallest, and easiest on Bill, who was the biggest and who could generally take it better.

There was one occasion when Pat had punctured a tin of condensed cream. It was just after the war and food products like that were very

---
3 From my mother, 1987.

hard to get. Mum had been collecting food for Pat to go on a camping trip. When she found the can of cream with the top perforated so the contents could be drunk she demanded to know who had done the evil deed. No one would own up so we three boys were lined up and, in turn starting with the eldest, were to receive three strikes on our bare bottoms with the leather strap until the culprit owned up. Three of the best from Mum was enough for me and just before the next three I claimed I was the offender, even though I knew I hadn't touched the camp food.

It wasn't until we were well into our twenties that Pat that finally confessed he had perforated the condensed cream can but was never going to confess, because he knew that if he did there would be no camping trip for him. As for me and my confession of guilt, I was told to pack my bag, put my coat on and go to the police station to report my crime. Fortunately my father returned home just as I was setting off down the driveway, so my visit to the police station was to be put on hold for 40 years.

THE HORSES OF HILL STREET
At Queen Street we had two horses, one called Jean—a retired show horse which pulled the two-wheeler gig (carriage) and the modern gypsy caravan—and the other was a gelded race horse called Don. He was reliable and sturdy but had a mind of his own, especially when we turned him around and headed for home. He would just take off, and my brothers who were the pilots and astute bareback horsemen, held on to the reins and mane for dear life. I'd hold on to my brothers and, if I fell off, I was determined Pat or Bill was coming with me. Don's next stop would be his tethering and feeding post across the road from our house.

Cotton reels were used for all kinds of interesting things back in those days. You could use them as floats on a fishing line or net or make any type of columned structure while playing with your blocks. Thus, they were big currency for a lad back then. I stole one from Mum's sewing machine drawer figuring she wouldn't notice. I took the reel away with me during a visit to town with Bill riding on Don; it was tucked away in the back pocket of my leather pants (which we were under strict orders to wear while riding). Things went well until Bill decided to head for home. Don suddenly clicked into gear and accelerated; I was left unawares and fell off Don onto the ground landing on my backside.

My mother later noticed her missing reel when she noted the bruise on my backside which had the very distinctive shape of a cotton reel. This time around she didn't give me any disciplining as she figured I'd suffered quite enough buttock trauma. Speaking of trauma, my longtime mate, the late Tony Clark whom I quote many times in this chapter, recollected our childhood together for this book. His recollections of unwittingly riding on Don, are priceless and rather scary

> The MacEwan family always had horses and one day I was invited to have a ride. Unlike my twin brother Dair, I played cricket in the weekends while he joined the pony club and later became an expert polo player. I was helped aboard the rather large horse and it set off at a brisk trot up Queen Street with me bouncing up and down on its back.
>
> The horse soon lost patience with this inexperienced rider and it bolted at huge speed on the chip-metalled road. I lost the stirrups, the reins and bridle and the saddle blanket started flapping. The faster it flapped the faster the horse galloped and by this time I was hanging onto its mane, fearful of the hard landing if I was to disembark. Finally it reached MacEwan's home and some green grass and it started to graze quietly. I stopped quivering long enough to slide off and I ran back to Neven with a sullied opinion of his mode of transport.

Later in the same year, Mum took us on a school holiday trip to Lake Rotoiti. We left with Jean and the gig plus two bikes, one of which was a tandem. To travel the distance 67 km today would take 50–60 minutes depending on your speed. Back then, our trip took four days. We camped on the roadside and took turns riding the bikes.

I was made to ride on the back of the tandem—just like when we rode Don—and was never allowed to take the helm. On one occasion Pat was on the front and I was in the usual position and we were going down a winding incline. Pat came to a corner he couldn't steer around and he yells, 'Jump for it!' My jump was hindered by the saddlebags packed around me. Pat then watched me careen into some blackberry bushes on the other side of the road and he laughed his head off. But I could see nothing funny about ending up deep in the blackberry bushes with scratches and sore from the bumps I had sustained when I finally stopped.

If the fog or mist came down when we camped at night, Jean would want company and she would back into the tent. Mum always got up and retethered her a little further away from the tent so we would not be disturbed through the rest of the night.

Whacked at Wellesley College

There were a couple of reasons why we boarded at the esteemed Wellesley College in 1944. The first was Grandma Mac (Dad's mother) who wanted her grandchildren to be in a safe, secure environment so badly she paid the school fees. The second was due to Dad being classed as unfit to serve in the New Zealand armed forces. Thus, the government considered his contribution to the war effort would be to work on a chicken farm in Upper Hutt. So we moved there to live with him in our horse-drawn caravan.

A famous proverb, 'The pathway to hell is paved with good intentions,' springs to mind. Grandma Mac's intervention was a disaster. My brothers were tougher and coped better than I did, but we detested Wellesley College.

It comes as something of a surprise when people meet me, expecting to hear stories of epic stoushes and dust-ups. You see, unlike many of my peers in Athletic, and All Blacks teams later on, who thrived on confrontation, I was never a hardman. Nevertheless, I do have one or two tales, one of which involves my accosting the heavyweight champion of New Zealand (this embarrassing and funny story comes later).

In fact I detested receiving and delivering violence, and I hated being in situations when I had to fight. If given the option in my childhood I would eagerly run away from aggressive individuals. I believe this came, in part, from my time at Wellesley when I was ten years old. It's not easy being a big kid: it is assumed you are tougher and more mature than you are. This means you'll get insecure kids wanting to test themselves against you. During these times I felt a great affinity with the children's story *Ferdinand the Bull*, though I dared not let on.

Due to my weight and size I was entered into the boxing championships. I actually did well in the preliminary rounds, but when it came to the finals against a very aggressive, trained individual, I was hit hard in the first round and never got to my feet again. I'm sure my brothers thought I had taken a dive and thrown in the towel. They might have been right, as I have never gone back into a boxing ring.

THE DENTIST DEBACLE

Call me old-fashioned, but I don't have a problem with the moderate and fair application of corporal punishment in schools. There have always been a number of nasty individuals who've needed a dose of reality. Sadly, corporal punishment became frowned upon thanks to sadistic traditions which didn't defend students from bullies, teachers from abuse, or control bad conduct in general. The bad eggs consistently punished otherwise good kids for trifling mistakes.

Suffice to say, I was subject to a particularly nasty case of institutional brutality which summed up my experience at Wellesley.

Bill had to go to the dentist, and he obtained permission to stay the night with Mum and Dad in Upper Hutt. In due course, I also had to go to the dentist and, like Bill, I also stayed the night with my parents. In my excitement I never got permission from the school. Hence, when I returned the next morning, they treated me like a runaway. I was caned in the headmaster's office, and again in front of the entire school. I was only nine years old and when my mother found out she wasn't pleased. I hadn't done anything wrong in her eyes and thus her baleful gaze was directed at Wellesley.

My mum was a highly territorial being who didn't like anyone, bar Granny Kerr, encroaching on her sphere of influence within the family. Thus, it was an anathema to her when Granny Mac called any shots concerning us boys. Mum now used our unhappiness as leverage to take us away from Wellesley at the end of the school year. So we returned to Richmond, and a new home in upper Queen Street.

Near the end of my time at Wellesley, Mum began taking on the Education Department over my early reading problems. They had begun well before Wellesley and became a rather unique feature of my early learning. Mum, had found me reading a book while holding it upside down; she realised I was reading from memory, not from any pattern of word recognition.

She was horrified when she realised my talent for recollection had helped shorten my time in the primers. My early teachers thought my reading skills were of a high standard and that I would cope in the next class up, but I had very little comprehension or concept of meaning, context, spelling or grammatical structure. Thankfully, by the time I reached Spring Grove and attended Wakefield School the situation had improved. So much so, my reports right through Nelson College showed great improvement.

Furthermore, I was lucky I'd been able to bluff my way through reading. An example of the treatment I could have received throughout my schooling occurred in 1945 at Richmond Primary School; it was straight out of Thomas Hughes' *Tom Brown's Schooldays*. Hugh Brown was the headmaster and I happened to be in his class on parts of speech and sentence structure. A sentence was written up on the blackboard – I can still remember the actual words: 'We were walking very slowly towards the edge of the road.' Hugh Brown turned from the board and asked me which word in the sentence was the verb. I just sat in my seat and said nothing and that seemed to make him very mad.

I was scared stiff so I called out the first word in the sentence: 'We!'

'We?' he said, almost choking on the words as he barked, 'Don't you know that a verb is a doing word? Come here and stand on my table and wee!'

Well, while I recall really wanting to take a leak, I was actually slapped around for no reason other than being a bit slow with my grammar. Brown was a good man, but he came from a generation of teachers who believed humiliation was the best means to learning.

My teachers were far more encouraging of my ability in mathematics. Indeed, the one thing which gave me any form of academic self-worth was my love for arithmetic, algebra and geometry.

Part II: Raising Richmond

In 1945, Mum and Dad purchased forty acres of property on Hill Street, a little further south of Freshfield. They planned to build a home there but the idea never eventuated. The land was heavily covered in gorse and a real fire hazard in the summer months. Nevertheless they decided that, with the right weather conditions, they would back-burn the gorse against the wind and firebreaks were cut in preparation for the burn-off.

A day of perfect conditions presented itself, the fires were lit and the burning began. It was going well when the wind changed direction and strengthened and the perfect burn-off turned into a raging inferno. Fences, power and telegraph poles were burnt and homes were threatened. The fire burnt for 24 hours but, fortunately, no homes or property were lost with the blaze. It was referred to ever after as the day the MacEwan boys set Richmond on fire.

Elmer Fudd & the Dynamite Kid

At this time Pat started experimenting with explosives. This sort of thing sounds positively crazy nowadays, but back then boys on 40 acres got up to all manner of crazy stuff. It was even more dangerous when you realise the war had been won, propaganda was at an all-time high and boys being boys sought to emulate the glorious deeds of the valiant allied forces.

The making of bombs was a direct result of what we'd read, heard on radio and seen on film. Out in the country we had access to wide-open spaces, and all manner of material: shotgun shells, fuses, fuse wire, nails, tin cans, the works. My older brothers Bill and Pat were great mates with Tony Clark and his brothers John, Bill and Dair. We fancied ourselves as commandos. It makes me laugh now, but Tony Clark's description below denotes how incredible it was none of us were blown to pieces or incinerated.

> We had three acres to play around in. A macrocarpa hedge grew up to the power lines near a roadside so we made up a gang, built a tree-hut complete with an escape hatch and we were allowed to have sleepovers. I should point out that, even after the war was over, my father commuted to Wellington for a year (via the two rusting ferries the *Arahura* and the *Matangi*) to assist editor Gilbert Joll write the history of the 23rd Battalion.
>
> For the four years that our father was away my mother was everything—a most successful multitasker, a staunch and steadfast Catholic, a fine cook and her housekeeping and gardening were tops. She played golf once a week with her close pal Linda Challies, and she became an enthusiastic connoisseur of our local cider. She was not a disciplinarian but we did most of what we were told because we loved her.
>
> Neven's family was also made up of four lusty boys and we got on well together so with a smattering of older brothers we were well equipped to deal to rival gangs who had the audacity to come onto our patch. Neven was a particularly welcome type because, as one member dealing with Churchill-like strategy, claimed that within our gang we had brains, muscle and speed! Our ammunition was dried-up cow pats and we were early developers of the Frisbee throw. Our favourite targets were large trucks passing on the nearby road. We experienced unrestrained glee when we scored

a direct hit on a tuba belonging to the Salvation Army band travelling on the back of a truck.

We reviewed our battle tactics in a forest about a mile away. As our tree hut attracted too much attention we organised a sleepout nearer to Neven's home and we were delighted to find long strands of passion-fruit vines ripening nicely along the banks of a pretty stream complete with a charming waterfall. Half-starved, dive-bombing mosquitoes plus the noise of the waterfall put paid to our outdoor sleeping so we reached home before our parents were awake. However our childhood was full of adventure and fun.

We found the ingredients of gunpowder and rammed the mixture up the hollow handle of an old saucepan. We made a fairly long fuse out of wax match-heads, lit the end and took cover as quickly as our speed would allow. We found out real early just what Guy Fawkes was all about especially as a piece of the handle went through a hedge and hit Neven's horse on the rump.

Pat seems to have been the catalyst for the bombs, and each of his explosive endeavours became bigger, louder, and more dangerous than the last. He soon had the bright idea of using me as a guinea pig for a rather spectacular demonstration on an unsuspecting willow tree. He ordered me to climb the tree while he bored holes in the trunk and plugged it with eight of his explosive devices.

He called out, 'Nev, are you okay?' I bravely replied I was. He then told me to climb up as high as possible, hold on tight and not move. I heard the match being lit, the hissing of the fuse, and through the branches I saw Pat scampering away as fast as he could. Like Elmer Fudd being taken in by Bugs Bunny for the umpteenth time I got this sudden sinking feeling in the pit of my stomach.

Boooooooooom. Craaaaaaaaaaccckkkkk.

The tree shook violently and split right up the middle. Pat was immensely pleased with himself, yelling, 'Nev, that was great.' I didn't share his enthusiasm; hence, it was the last time I ever took part in his explosives hobby.

EELS AND ARTERIES

On one occasion, we boys went eeling in the Waimea River, seven miles (11 kms) from Richmond. The shadowy pools there were a favourite haunt of eels, and every country lad pitted his wits against them with line or gaff. My older brothers had chosen a rather mean-looking gaff, with a wicked hook tied to a long handle. Unfortunately, by some mishap of boyish machismo, Pat managed to get the hook securely embedded in his leg and it wouldn't come out. It must have been incredibly painful. We were a long way from home. In a massive failure of brotherly oversight it fell to me to find a phone and contact Mum and Dad.

I got hold of my father but, either I failed to put the story to him properly, or Dad wasn't listening attentively. Either way, I clearly didn't understand sarcasm at the time for when Dad asked, 'What do you want—a stretcher party?' I replied enthusiastically, 'That would be wonderful.' However, no one came to help us.

I was annoyed when Pat wondered out loud whether I had stated his plight clearly enough. In reality Bill should have gone for the phone and explained the situation to Dad. In the end, poor old Pat spent three hours walking home with the gaff in his foot, lifting the handle up with each step. With hindsight I see that if he'd severed an artery it could have been curtains for him. Hence, my father felt a little guilty when we turned up at home.

Part III: Mother Nature's Son

We eventually moved to the farm 'Balgowan' at Spring Grove, which is between Brightwater and Wakefield. While Richmond saw me grow into a resilient and creative kid, it was Spring Grove where I transitioned from boy to teenager. So when I look back at Balgowan, I do so with much fondness, and a little sadness. I wouldn't reunite with the boy for some time.

I attended Wakefield School from 1947–48. I loved the life on the farm. It was great fun swimming in the summer in the Wai-iti River which ran through our farm. We built rafts, picnicked, and always went for a swim at the end of the day after harvesting tomatoes, or stacking the sheaths of corn stalks after the header had done its job. It was hard work but good fun. I liked everything about nature as a child. I thought flowers were the most beautiful of all. My favourite was the pansy. I have always found the colouring and presentation of this flower captivating. I thought the whole world ought to know of its beauty.

When I was 12 I shared these thoughts with my best friend. He roared with laughter and told everyone my favourite flower was a pansy. From that day I was called 'Pansy Mac' which hurt. I felt not only a deep sense of betrayal, but began to realise what a conservative society I had been born into. In my heart, I wanted to become some kind of artist and express myself in all manner of creative ways. One of those interests was music and I wanted to learn the piano. In 1947 I began learning the piano. I was given one for my birthday and I loved learning to play and enjoyed the progress I was making.

However, when I started playing serious rugby, going to music lessons again elicited scoffing from my peers. So much so, I gave the piano away. It proved to be a big mistake and is a deep regret I have had all my life. In trying to be what you think other people want you to be, you lose your identity, and your gifts. I dared not share my inner feelings about the arts and the gentler side of my nature any more. I saw it as a sign of weakness, and felt sure I would be ridiculed. Looking back now, it was a very sad state of mind to develop at such an impressionable age.

In 1949, a more stable family unit meant Mum and Dad fostered a boy David Froggart who lived with us for three years. David has some wonderfully vivid recollections of his time with us, which I shall share:

> Child welfare placed me in Nev's family's home and I loved every minute of it. I remember Neven and I ranged all over the Balgowan property. There was a whopping huge pine there and it was easily 100–200 feet up. We climbed the monster quite a few times. I was a

little more nimble and smaller than Neven so I could get higher up the tree onto the thinner branches. However, he didn't mind. Nev wasn't competitive; he was always more about admiring the view.

David also had fun joining us on fishing expeditions and, on one occasion, he helped remove a beehive from the farm without any protective clothing. His tale brings back fond memories of our safety standards. No one bothered to ask David if he was allergic, and luckily he wasn't. Yet, his story of bull-running while babysitting juvenile pigs and learning to drive is a particular highlight.

> Nev's mum took me for a driving lesson one day and we had a piglet in the boot of the car. Somehow, it managed to get out and into a paddock. I jumped over a gate to get it but I failed to notice there was a bull with enormous horns watching me run around. It decided to charge me. There was a bit of scrub in the way and I managed to get behind it. The bull was stomping around trying to get at me… This farmer, wholly unsympathetic to my plight, turns up and tells me in extremely unfriendly language to get off his property. So I had to make a run for the fence. I made it in the nick of time. It would have made for a great heroic story, but I was screaming and sobbing the entire way.

My hatred for guns was 'triggered' by a couple of experiences at Balgowan. One afternoon my foster brother David and I were alone at home and, as young boys at heart, were looking for something to do. Boys being boys we took the .22 automatic rifle off the wall and began to play the mildly disturbing game entitled 'Chase and Shoot the Hunted.' David was chasing me around the house; I could hear the automatic loading action and then the click and David saying, 'Bang! I've got you!' I turned into our bedroom and David came round the door from the hall and saw my reflection in the mirror. He aimed directly at the reflection and pulled the trigger. *BANG!* The gun went off shattering the mirror. I was a shaking mess. The bullet must have been stuck in the barrel and worked itself free before that final loading into the breech. It was the second time the gun had gone off accidentally. On the first occasion it had been hanging on the wall in the lounge. The jarring caused by our jumping in close proximity had released the firing mechanism. This event enabled us to explain in a plausible manner why it had gone off accidentally again.

GROWING PAINS AND JEANNETTE MOULDER
I was always solidly built. When I was born I weighed 10lb 7oz. I was almost 14 when things began changing. I'd always had a long body and relatively short, muscular legs, which had enabled me to run very fast. However, I started to shoot up, and the growing pains in my legs became extremely painful. Mum used to put hot packs on them to help soothe the pain, and they certainly helped. Quietly, Mum was quite relieved my legs had grown; she had worried I might have inherited my Uncle Neven's unnaturally short legs, a trait common in the males of the Kerr line.

This was not the case and, over the next two years, my body became well proportioned. I'd lost a bit of coordination, but I eventually regained it, and my running speed remained; indeed, it was augmented by a longer stride.

Nevertheless, Mum's relief at my growth caused another set of problems. Pat's shoes had been handed down to me until my growth spurt. My new body came with a catch. My feet were too wide to fit my brother's hand-me-down shoes. So I began going everywhere barefoot like we all had when we were in Richmond. When I started at Nelson College shoes and rugby boots were needed, and they were specially made for me by Spalding in Dunedin.

Yes, turning 14 was certainly a life changer; it meant I could begin playing rugby without either being left out of teams of my age—for which I was too big—or chopped up by teams because of my weight—for which I was too young. My growth spurt also combined with more primal developments.

When I started going to Nelson College in 1949 we travelled by bus picking up boys and girls along the way. The bus took the lads to

Nelson College and the lassies to Nelson College for Girls. The bus would start at Belgrove and travel through Wakefield, Spring Grove, Brightwater and Appleby.

The postmaster at Brightwater was Mr. Roi Moulder, and his eldest daughter was Jeannette. Jeannette attracted my attention right away. She was the best girl on the bus in my opinion, and we became quite friendly during the year. She was corresponding and seeing a bloke called Murray King. I knew this because I used to be their middleman taking letters from one to the other. Their friendship fell through, and I started to see Jeannette. It's a cliché, but it felt as if everything had fallen into place. It's pretty clear Jeanette felt the same way, for a time at least

> He used to bike down from Spring Grove to visit me and he impressed my mother, too, because he was so helpful round the house. He used to say, 'Can I sweep the yard for you, Mrs Moulder?' I remember a photo of him, when he would have been fifteen, leaning on a broom. He was so huge, and so gentle. He always treated me with complete courtesy – much more than most of the other boys. I remembered that later.

I used to bike to Brightwater in the school holidays. At that time Jeannette's father would let the exchange attendants take their holiday break and allow her to work one of the shifts. It was often the six to midnight one. The work would calm down in the evenings. I used to go down by bike to see her, or call in when driving home in our Austin car.

> We weren't supposed to entertain boys, but he didn't interrupt a lot of work after 9.30 pm, and we used to make toast on the exchange's heater. It was one of those two-bar electric ones with a safety grill over the elements—ideal for propping the bread on, as a generation of New Zealanders our age learnt. To go with it, there was coffee and thick, old-style milk from a tin.

I remembered those times in the telephone exchange making toast and coffee together and, while the journey home was sometimes cold and miserable if biking, it was all worth the effort just to be with her. The problem was I was 15, and in the Fourth Form. Jeannette was in the Fifth Form and sitting School Certificate. It was a social no-no for a girl to go out with a boy a year below, so she ended it. Jeannette recalls, 'I never saw him much after the fifth form year. The peer pressure got to me and it seemed to be the sensible thing to do.'

Obviously I didn't think it was sensible. I felt rejected, hurt and let down. Nevertheless, my ability to make a silk purse out of a pig's ear helped me channel my energy into my rugby, and other activities. Hence, I'd advise any young man or woman not to put a relationship before their passions and dreams.

Fifty Three as Good as a Hundred

A lot happened in 1951. My sport really began to take off. I also faced the dreaded School Certificate.

I was in Fifth Form. As well as developing as a rugby player I also achieved in other sports. I got a few placings in the senior swimming events and, despite my terrifying experience with firearms and my dislike of them, I found myself being something of a natural with rifles. I was so good with the damn things I ended up winning an award at school in my Fifth Form year. My old friend Tony Clark has a far better recall than I about my sporting achievements at that time.

> Neven also won a prestigious shooting prize (the Lady Godley Cup for .303 rifles) and the Senior Championship Shot Put. He performed really well in the cross-country races and showed overall that he was an athlete of outstanding promise.

Sergeant Major MacEwan

I'll interrupt my journey into 1951 with a brief look at my time of military training as a cadet during the August school holidays.

Godley Heads was well known for its three, six-inch, breech-loading Mark 24 gun emplacements. These cannons had been part of Lyttelton Harbour's WWII coastal defence battery. The Women's Auxiliary Army Corps were an integral part of the operation. These ladies manned the plotting rooms, mapped and sent coordinates of the targets to the lads at the business end. At a time when all they had were pencils, rulers and paper they were absurdly accurate. It always amazed me how at an elevation of 45 degrees, the guns could fire on targets 22 km away. When compulsory military training was abolished in 1958, the guns were scrapped.

At the cadet camp, I was appointed Company Sergeant Major. The appointment came as quite a shock to me, but people saw leadership qualities in me which had escaped my observation. Certainly, apart from my sporting ability, I was deeply unsure of myself and almost totally withdrawn socially. My position also gave me no end of anxiety: I felt sure I would really muck things up on parade and give the wrong order, consequently making a complete ass of myself. However this wasn't the case, and I came out of this very selective training camp with a glowing report. A sliver, a tiny nugget of real confidence grew in me for the first time in my life.

School Certificate

For kids of my era, right up until 2002, Fifth Form meant the dreaded School Certificate examinations near year's end. I was average academically, except for mathematics. I loved the subject in every form: algebra, trigonometry etc. There was something about the challenge and working out the answer through theorems, and formulas via a step-by-step process which really appealed to me.

Thus, I took Mathematics, followed up with Geography, Art, English (which was compulsory) and Science. I had learnt Latin when at Wellesley College, and I took French for the first two years at Nelson College. I was never a great linguist, and struggled with every aspect of sentence structure in English without attempting other languages. So French was dropped. The end of exams and the school year in 1951 left me feeling more than a little nervous.

I clearly remember awaiting the results. I knew the day they would arrive, and I stood eagerly at the gate of Balgowan for the rural mail delivery van. After hours of waiting around, I heard the rumble of the van, the shingle under its tyres. Soon enough an envelope was placed in my hot (not so little) hands; the date read 17 January 1952. I opened it up and looked at the statement… I'd passed.

I took off as fast as I could down our driveway to the house screaming my head off. Later on, it was Pat who felt the need to burst my bubble by telling me I had only scraped through with an average mark of 53%. Moreover, I had exceeded the minimum required mark for English by only four points. The subject which carried me through was Maths with a mark of 94%. Well, I'd certainly played to my strengths and, despite Pat's reality check, I'd passed. Fifty-three per cent felt as good as a hundred per cent.

Life as a boarder at Nelson College in 1952 certainly wasn't what I was expecting. Nor, was it top of my wish list. There were too many unhappy memories of my experience at Wellesley. Yet, thanks to my rugby experiences in 1951 my time training as an army cadet at Godley Heads, Christchurch, my self-confidence was improving. Lo and behold I could give orders and people seemed to enjoy taking my lead.

Part IV: Rise of the Gentle Giant

As a young bloke growing up it may surprise you that rugby was a bit of a mystery to me. I understood the basics of running, passing and tackling, but I was not a student of the game. I guess not many blokes are as kids. However, I think there were some lads who'd practised at least looking like they knew what they were doing. I had no such pretensions. I liked to see what all the fuss was about. Mid-game you would often would find me standing bolt upright in the middle of a ruck or maul looking around wondering, *What's going on.* Tony Clark, witnessed my mucking about and recalls I received some stellar advice which stood me in good stead.

> Our coach, Bernie Brown, insisted that Neven should keep his bum lower in the scrum and this advice was remembered right up to All Black days and beyond.

As it turned out I spent my time learning to survive against the older kids I was put up against due to my size. However, somebody had noted one or two things about my playing style and he came up to me one day and said, 'Nev, you've got an ability to jump for the ball in the line-out. Concentrate on that and everything else will fall into place.'

It turned out to be invaluable advice. I found I could do well in the line-out; I had the right sort of build. Moreover, my older brother Pat once shared an interesting observation. He'd obviously been thinking about our genetics and reasoned that, for solid blokes, we brothers had a lightness of foot and good balance other big lads didn't. He also noted, like the observer from the footy match, that I had the ability to jump.

Now, if Pat noted something good about you back in the day, you took notice. He'd been in the Nelson College first fifteen in 1949 and 1950. Pat had even found himself playing against Hutt Valley High School at Athletic Park in the curtain-raiser to the All Black versus British Lions Test. A very big deal indeed for Pat.

My first big push in rugby came when I was in the Fourth Form at Nelson College and Pat challenged me to continue the name of MacEwan as rugby players at Nelson College. I was a reluctant participant. I had never felt that I fitted into the world of thuggery, but I respected my brother's opinion of my skills and abilities. Once given an ultimatum to live up to the standard they had set, you damn well had too. I started to develop a sense of needing to prove to them I could achieve their ambition for the name of MacEwan to continue in the rugby records at the college. I envisaged getting battered by Pat for tackling practice. However, much to my relief it was clear Pat was getting enough of this sort of thing in training. Indeed, he was offering his assistance. So, making the most of this opportunity I asked if he would help me to understand the game.

I can recall Pat's reply almost word for word ...

> Look mate, there's two things you've got to get sorted. One is ball skills, and the other is your fitness. The ball skills, I'll teach you. As for the fitness you can run with me, but you've got to do it for

yourself. Then you can go to the coach, and see where he wants to put you.

Pat, was a gifted player. I spent hours every day practising with him. You name it we did it: passing, kicking, running onto the ball, jumping, good side, weak side, left foot, right foot, ball high, ball low—all of it. Fitness underpinned everything and we worked our backsides off. Near the start of the day we'd run around the block. In our rural neighbourhood the 'block' meant a series of country road junctions, maybe four miles from one intersection to the next. We got to run around it again after we'd worked on the farm. All up, we were running 32 miles (51 km) a day and, while we thought nothing of it then, just the thought of it now makes my feet ache.

THE TIN WING
At the end of 1951 Mum and Dad were considering selling Balgowan and moving to the North Island. So in 1952, I became a boarder at Nelson College for my sixth and final year of schooling. The boarding house I was allotted to was College House, a part of Fairfield House. The building was nicknamed the 'Tin Wing' since it was constructed from corrugated iron. It was an incredible place to be when it rained, the noise was deafening. Here I was reacquainted with my old French teacher Mr Brown who was now my housemaster.

I was put into the senior dormitory straight away. Although I was a sixth form student, as a first year boarder I was regarded as a junior student who needed to learn the drills, exercises and marches. I'd developed a good nose for such things as a cadet Sergeant Major; furthermore, the idea of getting up bright and early suited me. I was utterly dedicated to training by now and, being a senior, I could keep an eye out for any bullying or bad stuff. Indeed, I was well liked by the staff and my fellow students. I might have been a college prefect if I had stayed as a day boy in Monro House. The problem was Bernie Brown would never let me occupy any leadership role in Tin Wing; his reason was that since I was a new boy I had no experience of life as a boarder. Yet Tin Wing would play an important role in my development as a rugby player.

The food at Nelson College was pretty good. The records show that in the year I put on 11 lbs. Okay, the thought of melon jam and custard still make me ill today. Nevertheless, I was packing away the protein. I set the sausage-eating record by throwing down 24 snarlers in 30 minutes followed by a 100 yard dash. Rugby super-fan Granny Kerr supplemented my diet. I would make a regular trek to her flat in Bronte Street where I would wallow in girdle scones with boysenberry jam.

Due to my activities throughout the day I would sleep like a log at bedtime. I wasn't to know then, but my golden slumbers provided my growing muscles with an excellent window of recovery. Nevertheless, they'd also get a rude jolt. I soon discovered waking at 6.00 am for cold showers was not for the timid or easily embarrassed. The morning shower ceremony had a distinctly prison-camp feel. We were ordered up and herded stark naked into the showers. Even in the warm summer months they were terribly cold, so you can imagine how horrid our cleansings became during winter. No lad, no matter how proud, enjoyed the experience. The shrinkage was something to behold, and humbling to say the least.

The good thing was that the colder it became, the closer the rugby season was. My commitment to rugby grew and the hard training which had begun back in Fourth Form began to bear fruit.

PERSISTENCE AND PEN FRIENDS
My brothers thought very highly of Charlie Caldwell the Nelson College first fifteen coach. Pat sums his influence in this description:

> He could make a team. We had Guy Bowers in our side—the 1953 All Black. Other coaches built teams around Guy. Mr Caldwell built Guy into the team. People like Nev and me were useful to him for our size. I was fourteen stone at college. That counted as a big forward in those days. Nev was even bigger. Caldwell used to insist

on everybody having all the skills, forwards kicking with both feet, and so on. Well, it took hours of practice. You'd try to kick with your left foot, and you'd throw the ball up into the air and wind your foot up underneath it to try and hit it on the way down, and it'd dribble forward a yard or two and go nowhere.

When I presented myself to the first fifteen I saw myself as a worker. As long as I could keep a supply of line-out ball coming, I felt I justified my selection in the side. Yet, I had other aces in my possession. Firstly, I was jolly quick and agile for a bloke of my size. Wellington would make good use of these abilities, but the All Blacks would be a disappointment in terms of using my pace. By the 1960 tour of South Africa my coaches had learnt not to give me a ten-yard head start against our wingers in a 100 yard dash. Yet no coach ever made plans to use my skill set. Those who would have, like Dick Everest, were overlooked by the New Zealand Rugby Council (I'll discuss Everest and others later on). Thus, I do envy the way modern locks play the game today.

Secondly, thanks to my time spent with Pat, I had learnt to study all manner of forward play and this increased my confidence. With confidence came endurance, and with endurance, resilience. In rugby endurance and toughness are intimately entwined, mysterious companions. I played my heart out whenever I walked onto the field, but I was always the gentle giant. The calls of 'You need to be more rugged,' or 'Show a bit more mongrel!' echoed from my schoolboy days all the way through to South Africa in 1960. Sometimes, I thought they meant I should give more people a whack or be more filthy. There were times when I didn't know what they wanted at all. By the end of my career I didn't know who or what I was. However, thanks to my friend Doug Campbell, I found myself in communication with Tiny White, one of New Zealand's greatest lock forwards whom I idolised; I wanted to follow in his footsteps and dreamt that one day I would become an All Black like him.

Doug was one of our house prefects in the Tin Wing. Moreover, he was our school's winger and a huge fan of Ron Jarden, who by now was the Wellington and All Black sensation. Doug wrote to Jarden and asked for his advice about wing play, and he received many helpful replies. Among other things, Jarden talked of the value of accurate throwing in to line-outs—a winger's job in those days, before the hookers captured it in the early 70s. Jarden told Doug the skill was vital and must be mastered. He also told him of two kinds of practice: on his own, and with a mate. When he practised on his own, Doug was to make a mark on a goalpost and hit it repeatedly with the ball. The mark was to be on a post, not a wall, because this meant a miss would not bounce the ball back to the thrower. Doug would then have to walk for it, providing more motivation to become accurate.

When he practiced with a mate, Doug had to throw the ball to someone who jumped for it and returned it. One assumes Doug decided I was much more fun than a goalpost and promptly chose me for this exercise. I thought Doug's letter-writing was a great idea so I sent one off to the legendary All Black lock, Tiny White. I also received a reply, and I developed something of a pen-pal relationship with my hero. Tiny told me how he practiced jumping for the clothes line, for the crossbar of the goalposts and jumping past the point of being tired. Looking back Tiny and Ron Jarden must have had hundreds of letters per month from wide-eyed schoolboys like Doug and myself. Yet, the selflessness they showed us left a deep impact on me, and my interactions with younger fans followed their example. You can only imagine how I felt three years later when I was playing against Tiny and having Ron throw me the ball!

1951 Q̲u̲a̲d̲r̲a̲n̲g̲u̲l̲a̲r̲ T̲o̲u̲r̲n̲a̲m̲e̲n̲t̲

Before I discuss the tournament I feel it's time I addressed a nagging question I am always asked concerning my feet and rugby boots. I developed into a big lad. My feet were so large and broad I had difficulty getting shoes big enough to fit. Nevertheless, for the curious, my shoes and my rugby boots at College were specially made by Spalding in Dunedin. Indeed, Spalding would go on to supply my boots for the remainder of my career.

I left Nelson College at the end of 1952, after two years in the first fifteen adding to the MacEwan legacy. I also added a few extra achievements along the way. Nevertheless, the Quadrangular Tournament of 1951 played in Wellington at Wellington College, proved pivotal in my career. Everything we did during the rugby season culminated with this tournament which we played during the first weekend at the start of the holiday break after the second term. It was the biggest event on the sporting calendar for Nelson College.

The Quadrangular Tournament is the oldest inter-school rugby tournament in the country, played by four of the oldest schools in New Zealand: Wanganui Collegiate, Wellington, Christ's College (Christchurch) and Nelson College. On 14 May 1870, the first game of rugby in New Zealand was played between the Nelson Club team and Nelson College. Wellington College's first team captain, J Thompson, aware of Nelson's importance to the emerging sport in New Zealand, wrote in 1890 to Nelson College, Christ's College and Wanganui Collegiate asking them to participate in an annual tournament. Nelson College, the first invitee, declined—mostly due to the difficulties of travel and cost.

On 6 September 1900, Wellington College played against Nelson College for the first time. By 1925, Nelson committed to the competition and began their annual participation in the Quadrangular Tournament. Over the years, Wellington and Nelson Colleges have the best records of success. It has been very frustrating for this Nelson College old boy to see the Wellingtonians dominate the competition in recent times.

Thus, after the tournament in 1951, I was surprised to find myself the subject of an article which appeared in *The Dominion* likening my physical stature to the early Grecian Olympians. I was also surprised with the comment that they felt that I had shown potential to be a player of the future. In reality, I was just a schoolboy who loved to play rugby and win. My goals were to keep myself fit, be ready to give my all to the team and play to the standard I set for myself. So I was greatly encouraged by the feedback I was getting. It became the first item in my scrapbook on my rugby career.

NEVEN MACEWAN

3. My Career as a School Teacher

While I loved rugby, as you have read I had plenty of interests outside of sport and sadly, many had to be suppressed. Among these were my dream of flying commercial aircraft and owning a motorbike, dreams which had existed since my teenage years. I'd long been fascinated with aviation and I had applied to, and had been accepted by, National Airways Corporation, to become a pilot. One of my biggest regrets is I never went ahead with it.

My father told me there were two things I shouldn't do: have a motorbike and fly. The reasons he gave were that motorcycling and flying were so tenuous. If anything went wrong, that's the time you didn't want to be on or in either of them. Now, there's a lot of irony in this advice because Dad owned an Indian and did some hilarious things on it. Further, as discussed in the first chapter, he was a pilot and he loved flying.

WELLINGTON TEACHERS TRAINING COLLEGE
Apart from wanting to fly, I had no idea of what life after college held for me. However, late in 1952 there was an appeal for Sixth Formers to consider applying to train as teachers. The Education Department had fallen short on the number of their student teacher trainees for 1953, and they made a late-minute appeal for applicants. I thought, *Why not?* I made a late application and was accepted. Normally, applicants from Nelson would go to Christchurch Teachers College, but I requested to go to Wellington and to my amazement was accepted.

It's funny I should mention photography. It was during my time at Teachers College I became fascinated with film. Dad was a huge fan of 16 mm movies, and made several films promoting JB MacEwan & Co products for promotion and sales. Once again he was well ahead of his time in New Zealand corporate advertising. In 1930, he filmed the rugby test match New Zealand versus Great Britain at Athletic Park Wellington on 9 August and used the film to promote the company in rugby-mad Taranaki.

In 1957, on my first trip to Australia as a member of the All Black team, I finally bought an 8 mm movie camera. The footage I filmed of all the All Black tours I went on and my family as they were growing up have been enjoyed by everyone. My All Black tour films are held by Archives New Zealand in Wellington.

My time at Teachers College was one of great personal development and, since I was involved in various activities, I gained a real sense of belonging. I could now pursue my interest in drama, which started in Nelson College where I was a member of the drama club. Many years later as Public Relations Officer for Palmerston North I took part in the Christmas pantomimes. At Teachers College I was elected a member of the social committee. We promoted dances and other social events.

Initially, I lived in a private boarding house in Kelburn. In those days, Teachers College had their own rugby club and fielded teams in the Junior grade governed by the Wellington Rugby Union. I played for them in 1953. The coach was Jack Shallcrass who was on his way to becoming a noted name in educational circles. However, people are generally unaware of how good a coach he was. He really knew how to get the best out of his players. He certainly got the best out of me and I was selected for the Wellington Junior Representative Team playing four games for them. I must have been doing something right, because I received an invitation to play for the Athletic Club by one of the Junior Representative selectors, Des Bezzant.

It wasn't an easy decision to make: I had made a lot of great friends in the College team and I didn't like disappointing Jack. Nevertheless, when I approached him about the offer he told me it was a great opportunity and while he would be sorry to lose me he advised me to go for it.

ATHLETIC WAS THE RIGHT RUGBY CLUB
So in 1954 I began my 14-year association with the Athletic Rugby Club. Initially, it was hard to say if I felt I was improving. I wasn't a guaranteed starter for the first team, but I must have been doing well enough and it would have been hard not to improve given the calibre of teammates I had.

There was Nelson College legend Guy Bowers, at first-five. Guy and my older brother had played together in the Nelson College first fifteen. In 1953–54 Guy completed a tour of Britain and France for the All Blacks. He was partnered in the backline with fellow All Black and our halfback, Vince Bevan. They were a proper handful for opposing teams. Feeding Vince from the back of the scrum was 1950–51 All Black number 8, Graham Mexted from Tawa (Murray Mexted's father). My two immensely capable All Black trialist brothers, Bill and Pat were also in the team. (By way of digression, it mystifies me today that with the stars that were available to us we never became enough of a team to win the Jubilee Cup, Wellington's senior club trophy). Included among these top-drawer players was former Welsh and Lions lock, Don Hayward, now a Wellington prop. Don was one of the best all-round and shrewdest forwards of his generation. I'd also like to add (if anyone from Don's family reads this chapter) Don became a vitally important influence in the early days of my senior rugby career. He protected, encouraged and assisted me in every facet of my game.

Don had toured New Zealand with the British Lions' team of 1950. He liked it here so much he later returned to settle in Wellington. He had played at lock in three tests for the Lions, but we used his immense strength as a prop. This also saw him being used as a *line-out block*. Now, the name line-out block almost sounds like an American Football term. Yet, in the days before lifting in the line-out was legalised, props like Don would protect the big blokes like me leaping for the ball. Anything and everything could happen in a line-out back then, and anything and everything did. Don saved me from nasty incidents countless times.

An Unimpressive Start

Thanks to the Athletic team I earned my Wellington representative blazer by July 1954. Ron Jarden, like Don, played a major part in my wearing it. I would go on to play 134 times for Wellington until retiring from all rugby in 1967.

In my first training run with the Wellington senior team Ron came up and asked me, 'How, do you like it thrown?' I told him and he threw it there consistently. I could literally jump for the ball with my eyes shut; indeed, many times I had to (for a variety of unsavoury reasons). He could swing the ball across to my side without infringing the law and, to cap it off, he was left-handed which would have certainly made things awkward for lesser talents.

With him putting the ball right on the spot, and Don looking after me from behind, there was a great incentive to go. Other wingers I played with, especially later in my career, peppered me with the ball from all over—they didn't have the skills. Jarden was the best of them by a mile. Moreover, Jarden was the complete wing of his era. He could kick, he could pass and, oh boy, he was greased lightening on a break.

The first match I played in for Wellington was our second ever against North Auckland, a 16–16 draw in a rain-soaked, mud bowl of a game in Whangarei. Mum travelled all the way there to see me play, and I had a mixed bag of a game. When I got home I was called aside by Wellington's selector and coach, Clarrie Gibbons. He said,

> You've got a lot of football ahead of you Nev. It may not be this year, it may not be for a few years yet, but you're young, and you've got it there.

It sounds encouraging doesn't it? Yet, people forget rugby in New Zealand was ruthless in the amateur days. I got the message, loud and clear. I hadn't impressed the Wellington selectors enough in my first game and they were going to drop me. So in the next few weeks I had to play outstandingly well, above anything I had produced before, to make the selectors change their minds. My next two games for Athletic were excellent, and the Wellington selectors who were in attendance found it impossible to leave me out of the next Wellington team.

Clarrie's warning was the best thing that could have happened. By the season's final game, a 22–16 win over South Canterbury, I was a regular member of the side. After I had played against Wanganui at least one newspaper critic of the time was moved to comment that I was 'an outstanding jumper for the ball in the line-outs but there was 'a tendency to work him to excess.'

RUGBY FLATMATES

The people I met in the period 1954–1956 became highly important in later years. I had moved into a flat in Oriental Bay, not far from the band rotunda, which I shared with a couple of mates: Collier (Collie) Henderson and my old mate, Tony Clark.

> Neven and I were both accepted at Wellington Teachers College. We left behind our formative years in Nelson for the bright lights of windy Wellington. We shared a superb flat for a year right opposite the band rotunda along Oriental Bay with our diminutive halfback Collier Henderson.[4]

Collie gives a slightly more detailed run down:

> I had moved to Wellington from Taranaki and in 1956 I had a job teaching in Porirua. I joined the University Rugby Club. The coach was RB Burke; he arranged for me to teach at Rongotai College in Form One. Neven, it turns out was the Form Two master and we became firm friends straightaway. I was boarding in Grant Street, Wadestown, when another opportunity presented itself. Neven's parents were moving and Neven suggested I move in along with

---
4 Tony Clark, 2010.

him and his old mate, Tony Clark. We inspected an upstairs place overlooking the band rotunda with Oriental Bay a mere 100 meters away. We moved in. We share a lot of good memories.

Neven was playing rugby for Athletic Rugby Club, Tony and I for University. The rivalry was pretty fierce. Neven constantly reminded me what he would do to me if he caught me at the bottom of a ruck. I would reply, 'You're too slow; you'll never catch me!' One day he did! On top of me with others piling in, he said, 'Are you all right?'

I had to tell him, 'Yeah, you big wuss!'

Neven, Tony and I eventually all became Wellington representatives and toured together. Auckland, I recall was our first stop, Neven got injured. When I went to check on him in his hotel room, he told me the nurse was looking after him okay!

1955 – All Black Reserve

I made a lot of progress in the winter of 1955. Early in the club season, Athletic tried standing me off the occasional ruck or maul to bring my strength to bear on the burst. After one such match, a reporter noted, 'The use of the gigantic MacEwan as an extra attacking inside back did not constitute much of a menace to University.'

It would seem my bulldozing was average at best. In August, *The Evening Post* wrote a nice piece concerning my more conventional style of play at lock: '[MacEwan is] one of the finest lock forwards in the country, one who could walk into an All Black pack right now on his merits.'

Very heady stuff I must say, but momentum was starting to build. Wellington lost a home game 9–3 that year to Canterbury, the Ranfurly Shield holder. I felt gutted about the result as I thought we had worked them hard. I was a bit down about my role in the game. Whenever there was a loss I always felt partially responsible even if I wasn't the guilty party. The Canterbury pack was led by the established All Black lock, Bob Duff. After the game, the same critic who had praised me earlier reported I could 'at least break even against the formidable RH Duff. MacEwan's all-round play was magnificent.'

I was named as an All Black reserve in the series against the touring Australians in 1955. So here I was an All Black, a non-playing All Black, but an All Black nonetheless. Now, I am sure some readers' eyes are skipping back over the last sentence thinking how can you be a reserve, but be a non-playing All Black?

Reserves were there only in the case of an injury prior to the start of a match. We never stripped to sit on the bench waiting to replace an injured player as there were no tactical substitutions. The starting fifteen played the full game and, if anyone left through injury, you had to play on with however men your team had left. Consequently if you could still walk, you played on. Eldridge in 1950 is the classic example: he returned to the field and dived over to score the winning try against the 1950 British Lions with a broken collarbone and a gash above his eye, that required four stitches.

My initial reaction to being chosen was one of awe, but people like Don Hayward would give me some great lines to keep my head right, 'You're as good as these guys. You mightn't be as shrewd, but you're as good. You can do it; we're with you.'

Don was bang on. These blokes were shrewd players all right. I had lots of youthful enthusiasm, which was good, but many of my opponents at All Black level were not only able, they were smart. You can have all the skill in the world but experience is the major final ingredient, and there is no substitute for it. I had been lucky with Athletic and Wellington as I was surrounded by expertise and wiliness. I also had my schoolmate Don Campbell's hero Ron Jarden throwing me the line-out ball. This was one of the prime reasons I began catching the All Black selectors' eye. Moreover, I would soon be playing alongside Tiny White. My old mate Don must have pinched himself when he heard the news.

Alongside Ron, two other Wellington lads, a pair of flankers, also guided me into the All Black fold: Wellington's captain, Don McIntosh and a Nelson College old boy, Bill Clarke.

My Teaching Debut at Rongotai College

There were no big, formal graduations for teachers in my day. On 13 December 1955, the Wellington District Education Board informed me via mail that my teaching certificate would be granted by 1 February 1956. Most male teachers probably had a few beers with their mates when they became certified and you'd probably get a few handshakes from your colleagues. I don't recall the celebrations, but I do recall that 1955 had been a great year for me, and that I had a fantastic time at Wadestown School where I trained as a probationary assistant. I couldn't have had a better class; they were a great bunch of kids. If any of you young rascals are reading, you gave me the confidence to continue on in the profession.

Near the end of 1955, I was asked to consider applying for a position in the Intermediate Department of Rongotai College. The invitation came from the headmaster, Alf Lock, and the head of the Intermediate Department, Harry Guthrie. I believe I got the job not so much on my ability as a teacher, but as a promising rugby player.

Alf, Harry and the staff got to know me as an overly large, but rather good, lunchtime darts player, and not as some rugby bloke on the make. Hence, the comment below by Max Lane a fellow teacher at Rongotai means a lot to me:

> Neven was not an aggressive or abrasive personality as some forwards are. I always found him a very congenial colleague in the staffroom. He was very popular with Wellington crowds.

The staff at Rongotai were a great bunch of teachers. I know a thing or two about great teams, and they were a fantastic team. My feelings were shared and I'll quote one of the staff who became principal of a very large secondary school, who described my colleagues as 'the most invigorating, vital group of teachers I have ever been associated with.'

My spell at Rongotai College from 1956 to 1957 was my first experience of teaching in an Intermediate School which used streaming for classes from high achievers down to those who have difficulty achieving academic skills. Harry Guthrie asked me to consider taking the Form One boys with the lowest level of scholastic ability. I had no hesitation in accepting the challenge as Harry felt my being an All Black would help in motivating the boys in my class.

In accepting the challenge, I had no idea what issues I would face in developing a plan of learning within the set curriculum of the Department of Education. The boys in my class with little or no skill in doing the basics like reading and writing were hesitant to participate in discussions or group activities. Then there were others who had parents with high expectations well beyond their boy's capabilities. There were other boys who couldn't wait to get to their fifteenth birthday, leave school and look for a job. So I needed to come up with an activity which would capture their imaginations and inspire them to want to learn as well as developing the innate abilities and talents they possessed as unique individuals. So I was working on the initial strategy plan for the year when Harry Guthrie asked me to take the class for *two* years. I might add, I was really struggling to come up with activities I thought would work for one year let alone two.

Mr MacEwan and the 1956 Class Trip

The proposal I finally came up with and presented to Harry for approval was a week-long trip to Christchurch for the class. It would take place at the end of my second year. The lads would be required to plan their fundraising activities, sort accommodation, where they wanted to visit and what they wanted to do. Letters had to be written to obtain accommodation, visits to factories, Lincoln College, bus tours over the Cashmere Hills, city sights and beaches. The whole class wrote these and the best efforts were selected by the class as a whole and sent.

As they raised the finance for the trip I became aware of the boys' creativity both in generating ideas and implementing them. Their enthusiasm and effort was nothing short of infectious. There were bring-and-buy sales, competitions with an entry fee and cake stalls.

The major fundraising activity was delivering sample packets of Kellogg's cornflakes in the Wellington area. This project was a huge undertaking. I created work projects for the guys, and put them in groups of four. They had to count out the required amounts, and make a map of the areas they were going to deliver the packets. Their extensive preparation and planning ensured the task was successfully completed on time, and to the satisfaction of the company. Although I must admit some guys started to make 'airmail' deliveries, which was not acceptable. The packets had to be placed in the letter boxes and not thrown into the shrubs or onto the porches or verandas of houses! On the back of these efforts, the class of 1956 and I embarked on our trip to Christchurch.

I would meet many of the class members again after they finished their schooling. Catching up with them was always a delight, friends all. Through circumstance, I became closest with Graham Williams and Alistair Blair. Graham was selected to play for Wellington in 1964 while I was still playing for Wellington. The pupil was to become the teacher. 'GC' as he was known, was an outstanding player for the province, eventually playing some 174 games. I'll never know why he was suddenly dropped, and had such a short time in the All Blacks. He was selected in 1967, played 18 games in the Black jersey, and scored 18 tries which was an outstanding number for a loose forward then, and now.

Alistair, left college and joined the Athletic Rugby Football Club. He was a more than decent player, and I had the privilege of selecting him for the team that won the Jubilee Cup in 1965. He was an extremely popular member of the Athletic Rugby Football Club's World Touring Team in 1966. Alistair's recollections and those of his teammates can be found in my book on the subject.[5]

---

5 MacEwan, N. (2016). *Wellington Athletic Rugby Football Club World Tour 1966*. Palmerston North, NZ: Massey Printery. Copies are available from https://www.nevenmacewan.com

Harry Guthrie and I supervised the trip, but we also took along a senior boy to assist whom we knew was going to Teachers Training College the following year. We felt that assisting with the supervision on tour would be good experience for him; furthermore, his being a prefect and star player of the school's first fifteen would bring him respect. Thus, with the approval of the headmaster, Alf Lock, a student by the name of Mick Williment ably assisted us with the lads on the journey.

In the years to come, Mick and I were to share much in common. I taught at Rongotai until 1958, the same year Mick was plucked from the University Third Grade team to play for Wellington against Taranaki in our season finale. It was a stellar debut: he kicked five goals in a howling northerly to win us the game 23–20. Mick later followed me into the national team. Like Graham, he would be dropped from the squad, and no one in the country comprehended the decision. Soon after, he became a partner in my firm Nev MacEwan Travel Ltd.

NEVEN MacEWAN

4. Rugby Tests and Jerseys

MY FIRST TEST FOR NEW ZEALAND 4 AUGUST 1956

I had stirred from a good night's sleep to the sound of the wind whistling around the Midland Hotel, which told me my first test match for New Zealand was going to be played in bleak weather. I had hoped to play on a fine, sunny day similar to the conditions I'd played in against the Springboks for Wellington a few weeks earlier.

I was rooming with the great Waikato prop, Ian Clarke. Ian had been captain of the All Blacks in Dunedin in 1955 playing number 8 against Australia. I had been selected as a reserve for that game. The selectors felt it was appropriate for me to share a room with Ian so he could mentor me in my preparation for the test.

I started going over the game plan, the line-out calls, where I would position myself for the kick-offs, my expected running lines from both line-outs and scrums when on defence and where I needed to be positioned when we were attacking. Other than set play, which you couldn't really plan for, I had to trust my natural abilities and experience as a player.

MY MATCH DAY ROUTINE

My prematch routine was well and truly established, and it would serve me well throughout my playing career.

Breakfast was the important meal on a game day. It would consist of a cereal, bacon and eggs, toast and coffee. After breakfast it was time to get my gear ready for the match. My boots always had to be cleaned and polished. My laces had to be spotless, so too my shin pads, jock strap, shorts, jersey, headgear, and my socks and garters. They were all folded and packed into the kitbag ready to depart for the game. I'd double-check every time to ensure every item was there and in perfect condition.

The preparation took me about an hour and a half. The great thing about it was that the physical activity enabled me to focus with greater clarity on my skills and what the team expected me to contribute to the game plan. For me, the important preparation for any match was to know my opponent, but to focus on my skills and expertise to beat him in every aspect of the game.

Athletic Park Changing Rooms in 1956

By the time the team got to Athletic Park, the weather had deteriorated. Terry McLean wrote in his book, *The Battle for the Rugby Crown*, that the swirling southerly gale built up to 48 mph (77 km) by match time. McLean reported during the game that the wind had dropped down to 20 mph, but the gusts of wind, which rattled through were easily in the 40s. I agree with the rugby experts then and now about the weather giving the public false confidence. Wellington's often wild winter climate has always been difficult for teams used to playing on firmer or drier ground, like South Africa and Australia. Also, it is important to remember that the drainage of the grounds was very poor at that time—nothing like the grounds of today. Our changing facilities were also a challenge for both teams.

In 1956, New Zealand's facilities for rugby were extremely poor. I shudder to think what the Boks made of them. Indeed, anybody playing representative rugby in my era and well into the professional one will tell you that Athletic Park's changing rooms left a lot to be desired.

The stark, perpetually freezing, dank, concrete rooms we changed in on the day were part of the foundations directly holding up the old main stand. You could hear the rumble of the crowd echoing above you. The changing room had just enough space for the team, and the shower room and toilets were in a little room off the main changing area.

Clearly, it was a terrible place to change and prepare for a match. The after-match social area also had very limited space and offered only very basic facilities. Present-day test players have no idea the conditions that were offered to teams in those days. But you made the most of what was available. Sometimes after a game the run on the hot water would see some players who were late to the showers having to have a very quick, cold shower. When an international match started the coaches were not allowed to make any contact with the team until the final whistle was blown and, at half-time, teams were not allowed to leave the field. When the teams ran onto the field the captain was totally in charge, making the calls and changes to the game plan.

My First Test – 1956
In the second test against South Africa in Wellington we played with the wind in the first half and managed to get the first try of the match via Bill Gray, but we wasted a lot of effort. By half-time, we had only one score to our name. I remember Bill Clark, Don McIntosh and I exchanging a few frustrated glances as we kicked, kicked, kicked, and kicked some more. Tiny White and Bob Duff were fighting really well for the ball in the line-outs, but it was for nought. I started out well enough, but I soon found myself grappling with Johan Claassen; he was everywhere I didn't want him to be.

Ron Jarden played the worst game of his esteemed All Black career. He missed touch kicks, crucial penalties, and conversions that he would usually have knocked over in his sleep. I also have to spare a thought for our halfback and captain Pat Vincent. South Africa was so good at disrupting our line, and surrounding our rucks and mauls that when we won possession we couldn't give Pat and Mick Bremner the space and protection they needed. In the second half Lochner, who had terrorised Pat and Mick, now went after Bill Gray.

Bill Clark and Ron Jarden had developed a fantastic understanding playing as they did for the same club and provincial side. Ron would kick infield from the touchline after a backline movement and Bill would either give chase down the centre of the field and pressure the opposition's backline or, more often than not, catch it and punch upfield. Bill was a wily fellow, very strong; he had a big tank, and could be pretty quick in short bursts. Hence, for every wayward kick Ron made, Bill still constantly tracked the ball. As a result the Boks struggled to close Bill down and he became one of the few who put regular pressure on the Bok's line throughout the game.

One of the other heroes of the day was Morrie Dixon of Canterbury. I rated Morrie highly as a competitor, and so did the Cantabrians. Sadly, he is another fellow who didn't get the recognition he deserved from the selectors or the New Zealand public. Morrie wasn't quite as quick or skilful as Ron, but I'd really grown to admire his skills as a line-out thrower during the countless extra practices we had prior to the second test. He was a great tackler and an incredibly feisty scrapper. He was also the master of the wind-up. A highlight of the match was when he called Paul Johnstone 'yellow', which, in twenty-first century terms, means a coward. In those days it was one of the worst things you could call a man and it set Johnstone off. Morrie and my Wellington teammate, Don Hayward, turned out to be my greatest teachers in the art of niggling. If you could cause your opponent to worry about you, then you'd won. If he got to fighting you, even better; it meant he'd clearly been rattled and was focused on you rather than his team's game plan.

We limped back to the changing room. Down the hall the winning Springbok team were well pleased; their spirits were up and they were celebrating their victory. Our mood was as sombre as the weather. Nevertheless, some wonderful things came out of this experience.

1956 – THE AFTERMATH
The selectors were always reviewing and assessing individual player's abilities and making changes they thought would improve the team's

performance. I did not play well enough to retain my position in the playing fifteen but was retained as a reserve. *The Evening Post* referred to me as 'a young player, making his international debut in a totally unaccustomed position, [and who] was not surprisingly unsure of himself on Saturday.'

McLean, in *The Battle for the Rugby Crown*, called me 'a magnificent physical specimen who had not shown, as yet, the toughness nor the cunning and craft of the ideal test forward.'

Headlines like that didn't bother me. I was part of the reserves for the entire series so I continued watching, learning and helping out the team selected to play on the day. I felt very much part of the team. It's a curious thing when you're part of an elite squad, but still a fan of the game at heart. I was as excited as everyone else when Don Clarke, Ian's brother, was finally selected for the All Blacks. He was joined by Peter Jones and Kevin Skinner. Kevin Skinner played for Otago but he was also the New Zealand heavyweight boxing champion in 1947. He was greatly respected as a player; you certainly didn't want to try and put one across him. If you did you would come off second best. I know from experience.

My Encounter With Kevin Skinner

In my first season playing for Wellington on our southern tour we played against Southland, Otago, South Canterbury and Canterbury. In the match against Otago, there was this guy in the line-outs who was being very disruptive and making things very difficult for me to jump cleanly for the ball. I turned to Don Hayward as I always did when I was receiving interference when jumping for the ball and said, 'Don, fix him!'

Don replied, 'You're a big boy now. You fix him yourself!'

I had to stop this guy from disrupting my line-out jumping. Don Hayward had made it quite clear he was not going to do anything about it. So at the next line-out on our 25-yard line I let fly with a wild punch which missed the offender. The swing was duly noted by the referee and I was penalised. I found myself under the post deeply frustrated as Otago prepared for a shot at goal, when Don came up to me, and said: 'You silly boy. Do you know who that was you took a swing at?'

I replied, 'No.'

Don shook his head. 'That's Kevin Skinner, the New Zealand heavyweight boxing champion!'

Don and Kevin were very close mates. Don was Kevin's best man at his wedding. So I was set up by Don and the three of us would entertain people with that incident for years.

1956 – THE THIRD TEST
The All Black selectors made seven changes for the third test in Christchurch on 18 August 1956. Waikato's fullback Don Clarke replaced Pat Walsh; Robin Archer replaced Mick Bremner at first five-eighth; Ponty Reid replaced Pat Vincent at halfback; Peter Jones replaced me at number 8; Tiny Hill replaced Don McIntosh on the side of the scrum; and Ron Hemi replaced Denis Young as hooker. But the most significant inclusion was Kevin Skinner who replaced Frank McAtamney in the front row. Walsh, McIntosh, Young and myself were retained as reserves.

Kevin Skinner had not been available for All Black selection since the tour of Great Britain in 1953–54 and took no part in the 1956 All Black trial matches. He was called into the third test side to strengthen the front row and support play in the line-outs. Kevin Skinner was a truly outstanding prop forward, one of the all-time greats. He could play either side of the scrum with ease; he had strength, technique, a good head for the game, and boy, he was dependable in the tight.

It's well known that Skinner gave Koch and Bekker a torrid time in the third test. During the match Ian Clarke and Kevin swapped sides in the scrum and there were all sorts of stories told about the change. One was that Ian was having trouble with his severely cauliflowered ear. The simple explanation was that Kevin hadn't appreciated the tactics used by Koch and Bekker in the second test and the attention they gave Frank McAtamney in the first scrum. He also had a few scores to settle from the 1949 tour of South Africa. Did that sort of retaliation go on in rugby in the 60s? Of course it did, but it was very seldom seen. There were no television cameras or Television Match Officials or instant replays at test matches then—just the referee. So there was always an opportunity to correct a player who persisted in playing 'the man' rather than the game. Skinner never went looking for trouble. If anyone was not playing the game he would give them a warning—just one. If the offender persisted he would give them a short, sharp, powerful punch and the matter was resolved.

This was the test in which fighting was first seen but fortunately we had a good referee in Fright, from Canterbury, who was always in control of the game.

The New Zealand forwards all played well that day but Tiny White, playing his twenty-second consecutive test, stood out. The man of the match that day was Don Clarke; with his line-kicking and goals you just couldn't fault his effort. It was a complete performance for his first test.

Unnecessary Brutality

The Springboks had one of the game's greatest thinkers and strategists at that time, Danie Craven. He had developed his team's skills and they were smart, clever players of the game. But I couldn't make sense of the Springbok's 'extra' tactics. They were constantly playing the man even when winning comfortably. Koch and Bekker, the two hard-as-nails South African props, had taken care of Mark Irwin in the first test. Their target in the second test was Frank McAtamney. Frank was punched and lifted right out of that first scrum. I was thankful to be at number 8 when I heard the impact. But that was what we had come to expect from the South Africans by then. They wanted to win at all costs.

I never bought into the argument put forward by some sports writers and Springbok players that their negative play was due to being handled roughly in the provincial matches. While I have no doubt they were given a tough time. I think Kiwis of my generation have been too polite on the issue of cheating. It was part of the game then and still is today. You are trained to go to the limits of the law and sometimes that results in actions and criticisms that puts the game in a bad light.

An Audience With Dr Craven

A couple of years before the 1956 tour, a young and highly talented Springbok centre from the 1953 series against Australia, Danie Rossouw, announced his retirement from the game. He gave as his reason the undue emphasis placed upon sporting achievement. In his opinion sporting recognition had crossed the line into idolatry. Today, as a Christian I can relate to Rossouw's comment.

I first met Dr Danie Craven after the Springboks' game against Wellington and I would go on to meet him many more times over the years. At the end of the Springbok tour, he spoke on the topic of 'Christianity in Sport.' Danie was an incredibly smart, charming, charismatic figure who, up until 1956, was the most dominant figure in world rugby. His celebrity status in New Zealand was immense and he drew large crowds. He lamented the playing of sport on Sundays and also discussed how sport suffered when it became about winning at all costs. Craven saw sport as a celebration of humanity. He saw rugby in its pure form as a work of art.

If the 1949 team to South Africa had read or listened to his speech they wouldn't have been amused. If Irwin, McAtamney, Jarden, Gray and Tiny White had heard Craven's comments about the dangers of winning at all costs, they wouldn't have been amused either. Craven described beer and bets as social evils and the irony of his statement was that our national pastimes in the 1950s were rugby, racing and beer.

Danie Craven was correct about the social evils of our sporting culture of that time and it hasn't improved in our so-called enlightened times of today. I know first-hand how empty and damaging our alcohol culture can be and I know I'm not the only one. Wellington's former captain, BJ Lloyd, made some very profound comments on the subject. BJ had retired a year before I'd shown up in the squad. He was honest and thoughtful; a man who had played 72 times for the province and captained the 1953 Ranfurly Shield winning side over Waikato. BJ had long been concerned with the alcohol abuse he saw around him. In late September of 1956 he was quoted as saying, 'If a player cannot give up the beer, he should stay with the beer and give up his rugby.'

In the wake of our series win BJ's message would have been overlooked by many of us. However, time proved BJ more than correct. While my struggles with alcohol, which began in South Africa, would one day become national headlines, I failed to recognise the reasons for my drinking. I know more than a few potentially great players that alcohol laid low and many successful players who fell victim to it when their playing careers ended.

1956 Shield Challenge
With the departure of the Springboks and New Zealand's place as rugby's number one nation finally secured, there was one big task left for my Wellington side: winning the Ranfurly Shield on 22 September. To get hold of it we had to take on the mighty Springbok-beating Canterbury side. The Cantabs had thrashed us to win the shield in 1953 and had held it against all comers ever since. We had challenged once, seeking to wrestle it back in 1955, but they'd routed us 30–11. The 1955 defeat was hard to take as our team had been fancied to beat them.

In the aftermath of the Springboks we all felt a little flat. So flat our form nose-dived. After our narrow loss to the Springboks we'd gone on to be beaten by NZ Universities, Wanganui, Taranaki, Auckland and Southland. We had also lost our point-scoring machines in Ron Jarden and Tom Katene. Canterbury weren't worried about us in any way shape or form. What they didn't take into account was that they believed we would play our usual expansive game. The game plan developed by our assistant coach, Vince Paino, was the exact opposite. We played the 10-man game. That meant we played the game with the eight forwards plus the halfback and first five-eighth and playing the sideline or into 'the box' which was the area behind their forwards and the area between the fullback and blindside wing.

We liked to run the ball through the backline. However, Canterbury was more conservative and had a reputation for a strong forward pack, a crash-tackling midfield, and exploiting their opponents' errors. In turn, Canterbury's observers had watched us play our free-flowing game against South Island teams. Paino's plans were finalised in Timaru before the team got anywhere near Christchurch. In due course, Ivan Vodanovich, Ian McIntosh, Bill Clark and I took Canterbury on up front which meant taking on fearsome blokes like Bob Duff, Tiny Hill and the gang.

The match and Paino's tactical genius were reported in *The Dominion:* 'Close marking and resolute tackling saw Canterbury falter under pressure.'

The Evening Post explained, 'It may not have been magnificent, but it was war—war, anyway, in the rugby sense.' That describes the type of game Wellington played in beating Canterbury 8–0 to win the Ranfurly Shield. The Post's report added that the Wellington players, 'did what they had been asked to do and did it like heroes.'

It was reported that my contribution to the game was 'tops— international status in everything he did, especially in the line-out.'

We hung on to win the game 8–0. Alan Clark our number 8 scored the try and Kara Puketapu kicked a superb conversion from the sideline. Jim Johnstone kicked a penalty to seal it. Some Canterbury voices rather hypocritically criticised Paino for his choice of tactics. He remarked, 'When in Rome, do as the Romans do.' It was clear the Romans didn't anticipate a taste of their own medicine.

My first test match for New Zealand was very special and I swapped my first test jersey for Springbok captain Basie Vivier's one; it became a very treasured memento. In 1974 this jersey, along with two other very special test jerseys started their journey to Wales, to the town of Cylfynydd about 30 km north east of Cardiff. The Springbok jersey is still on display in the Cylfynydd Rugby Club's Trophy cabinet. The other two very special jerseys returned home to Palmerston North some 37 years after they were given to Joe Rooney in a gesture of goodwill to cement ties between the people of a small town in Wales and New Zealand.

1959 – THE LIONS TOUR
The second test jersey of importance was from the 1959 British Lions tour of New Zealand. In the first test against the British Lions played in Dunedin on 18 July we were very fortunate to come out the winners by 18 points to 17. The tourists scored four tries: one to Tony O'Reilly, two to Price, and one to Jackson. Rissman had one conversion and Hewitt got a penalty goal. Don Clarke kicked the now-famous six penalty goals to win the match. In the second test played in Wellington on 15 August 1959 New Zealand won by 11–8. While the winning margin was small, New Zealand deserved the victory scoring three tries to one, two being scored by Ralph Caulton. Don Clarke again added extra points by scoring the third try and adding a conversion. New Zealand comfortably won the third test 22–8 on 29 August 1959. We scored four tries to the tourists' one and our approach to this game was motivated by an article that appeared in the Christchurch press written by Vivian Jenkins. The article was not complimentary to the New Zealand side concerning the way they had achieved the victories in the first two tests. Innuendos were also directed at what he had thought was biased refereeing.

Vivian Jenkins, rugby reporter for London's *The Sunday Times* went on to write in his book,[6] *Lions Down Under* that:

> The third test was a triumph for New Zealand. Their forwards gave a tremendous display, one of the finest in their country's history, and the result, a win by 22 points to 8, in no way flattered them. Indeed the margin might have been even greater, for they attacked for almost the whole of the second half, and could well have scored

---
6 Vivian Jenkins (1960) *Lions Down Under* (p.225) London England, Cassell and Company Ltd London

two or three times more. For the Lions, of course, the opposite applied. This was the low ebb of their fortunes. They had lost the series, three-nil, but more than that they had been outclassed on the day, and made to look a thoroughly inferior side.

I played only three test matches against the 1959 British Lions touring side. The two British Isles locking opponents were Rhys Williams and Roddy Evans, two great locks from Wales. I rate them in the top five lock forwards that I played against in my international rugby career. After the third test[7] Roddy and I swapped our playing jerseys.

I missed the fourth and final test through measles and Roddy was not available through torn lateral ligaments in his left knee sustained in the match against the New Zealand Maoris played on 5 September 1959. Roddy flew home before the tour ended for specialist treatment.

1960 – The South Africa Tour

I obtained the third test jersey on the tour of South Africa in 1960. I wish to comment on three matches played on that tour. I was privileged to be appointed as captain for two of them in addition to the last test played in Port Elizabeth.

I wore the third test jersey of significance in the fourth and final test against South Africa in Port Elizabeth. Going into that test match the series was all tied up: the first test had been won by the Springboks, the second test won by New Zealand and the third test resulted in an amazing draw. The scene was set for the showdown and South Africa desired to win the series to put the records straight and even the score of the loss in New Zealand in 1956.

South Africa won this match 8–3, but we assisted them with that victory by a team selection which, logically, had no sound basis. The same errors that the 1949 side made were repeated (and the same errors continued to be repeated until 1970 under the coach Ivan Vodanovich). All three tours highlighted the weakness of the Rugby

---

7 See Appendix C 1 for match details.

Union appointing people to key positions based on the 'old mates' basis rather than choosing the best coach available at the time. For example, in 1949 Vic Cavanagh (Otago) should have been the coach on that tour but the New Zealand Rugby Union (the 'council of learned men') thought and decided differently. However, in 1960 Jack Sullivan was appointed. He was a great player and businessman but lacked the ability to assess and think outside the box. Dick Everest should have taken the team following up the successful tour with the All Blacks to Australia in 1957 and having been a member of the selection panel for the 1960 tour. The other contender for coach was JJ Stewart (Taranaki) who had taken the Colts tour to Ceylon in 1955. On that tour he was not only coach, but also manager and baggage man all wrapped up in one. The irony was that Stewart would show his abilities with Taranaki in the great Shield era of the 1960s and he eventually became the All Black selector and coach in 1975, twenty years after taking the Colts team on that very successful tour of Ceylon.

In 1970, Ivan Vodanovich was appointed to succeed Fred Allen even though Fred was the man for the job. Just as in 1949 when the New Zealand Rugby Union had it in for Cavanagh, in 1969 the New Zealand Union, under the chairmanship of Jack Sullivan, had it in for Fred Allen. Strange as it may seem the New Zealand Union appeared to look for any excuse to remove successful coaches, especially those who had flair, insight into the game and that X factor that got extra mileage out of players. Wellington had such a man: Bill Freeman. During my 14 years of playing for Wellington he was without doubt the best coach Wellington had. He was very successful; his record speaks for itself. Ironically he never made the All Black selection panel nor coached the All Blacks. On the other hand Ivan Vodanovich, who had never coached a provincial team as a sole selector, was appointed to the All Black selection panel and was coach of the 1970 All Black team that toured South Africa. It was not surprising he was eventually shown to lack the skill to mould players into a team or enable a team to function beyond their existing level of expertise. Ivan took over from Fred when the Union pushed him out and coasted on the team's ability to continue the playing style that Fred had developed. But his staid, stagnant and limited approach resulted in the 1970 tour of South Africa being a disaster. There is no doubt in my mind that if Fred had taken that touring party to South Africa New Zealand would have won the series that year.

I believe that we had the team in 1960 to win the last test in Port Elizabeth but we selected the wrong players for the game and paid the price for our error. The commentaries on the team's selection are interesting. It is often said that hindsight is all very well, but a good coach sees ahead and makes the hard calls that meet every known factor. The X factor is building confidence of character and self-belief into his players, that no matter what happens they are as good as the opposition, that they will stand their ground and, with their collective skills, excel and defeat their opposition. Attitude and choices are the ingredients that eventuate in success.

It was my belief that we should have won the last test and I decided to keep my All Black jersey as a memento. The ground we played on was very significant for me.

During the tour I had the enormous privilege of captaining the team on two occasions. The first game was the match before the first test when we played Northern Transvaal. Danie Craven had informed me that this was going to be the teams fifth test. The Northern Transvaal side was reputed to be the best in South Africa at that time. We won that match comfortably with a display of rugby that was outstanding.

We were fit, focused and committed to the task and everyone played great rugby with Peter Jones in excellent form. This performance gave the team real confidence going into the first test the next week in Johannesburg. Daan Retief, the grand loose forward of the 1956 New Zealand tour, rated Peter Jones's performance that day as the best of any international forward playing at that time. For me personally the performance of Dennis Young was the greatest. I know he will correct me if I'm wrong, but he took nine *tight heads* (hooks against the put-in) in the game, an outstanding achievement in any international match. Salty du Rand was the coach of the Northern Transvaal side and he was surprised at the defeat handed out by the All Blacks, especially considering the calibre of some of his players.

There was no doubt in my mind that Salty du Rand was still hurting from the 1956 defeat in New Zealand and the memories of the tough, rugged forward encounters he experienced on that tour was uppermost in his mind approaching this game and his strategies for the game.

Loftus Versfeld was the venue for the match; it held a capacity crowd of 42,000. Thousands of children were accommodated in the arena for the match.

I remember two things from this match. The first was the comment made by the referee, Mr Hofmeyer, to Jaap Bekker. After a minor forward skirmish Jaap was left writhing and groaning on the ground; he was throwing a 'Hollywood' worthy of an Oscar award. But the comment from Hofmeyer was in effect, 'Stop your squealing, Bekker, and get up. This is a man's game.' Great stuff and a great referee. One of the best we encountered on tour.

The second incident was the blatant boot to Kevin Briscoe's head by Vermaas, which left Kevin out cold. In the modern game he would be cited and, without a shadow of doubt, would be banned for life. Kevin responded to a good dose of 'smelling salts' and, while still very groggy, continued to serve the team until the final whistle.

The Transvaal crowd started to get very frustrated with the scoreline and some of the heated exchanges between players and the booing and yelling, particularly when Don Clark was taking a shot at goal, were disgusting. After the match, Ian Balfour, the English-speaking South African commentator, said he was ashamed to be a South African on account of the crowd's behaviour.

I will remember this match as the ultimate display of great forward play and dominance by the All Black team.[8] The three outstanding

---

8 See Appendix C 2 for match details.

forwards for the All Blacks that day were Dennis Young, Peter Jones and Dave Gillespie. In the back Kevin Briscoe deserved a DSM, while others to make their mark were Adrian Clarke, Don Clarke, Terry Lineen and Kevin Laidlaw.

The tactical approach to the game by the Northern Transvaal team was regrettable because their negative approach to the game nullified the players of great ability in their team, such as Stompie van de Merwe, Vermaas, Bekker and de Klerk.

The other game of which I was appointed captain was against Eastern Province played at Port Elizabeth at Boet Erasmus Stadium. The game was a shocker and has become known as the 'Battle of Boet Erasmus'.

The referee lost control of the match, and blatant playing the man by the Eastern Province resulted in very little constructive rugby being played. Jack Sullivan commented that after the game the All Black changing room 'was like walking into a World War II casualty centre.'

At half-time my comments to the team were very simple and, I think, to the point: 'Everyman for himself and I'll see you in the dressing room after the game.'

I asked the referee Mr Carlson after the match why he hadn't stepped in and penalised the blatant thuggery. He astounded me with his reply; he stated, 'I knew who started the trouble and so I was not going to penalise your blokes for retaliating.'

When the scrum formed and the front rowers went down against each other Holton would go straight into Eric Anderson, our prop, with his head. Head hitting head. Not a pleasant sound. Our backs were tackled late and taken out of play both after and before they received the ball. In my opinion it was as if the Eastern Province side had gone out to deliberately soften us up. One of their players was reputed to have said that we could not mix it with them when it came to hard Afrikaans rugby. Well they were sadly misinformed. I remember asking 'Kudo' Anderson (Eric) if he wanted to shift prop position with Ian Clarke and he replied with his battle scars showing, 'No, Nev. I'm all right. I've just about got the measure of him.'

Why did we have such a referee? Well you have to remember that on that tour of South Africa in a sense *we* appointed the referee to control our games. That might seem a strange statement, but the touring team was given a list of three referees for a match and the team would select a referee from those names. The touring team could make enquiries about the referees, and this was done, But it was not always possible to get good advice, or advice that was not biased one way or another. We were given a list with the names van der Merwe, van Rensburg and Carlson; it was logical to assume that one of the men could be of English heritage and, on that assumption, Carlson was appointed. But his refereeing skills left a lot to be desired.

Another aspect of international matches at that time was that there were no replacements. The starting fifteen had to finish the match and if a player had to leave the field of play on account of injury there was no replacement; the team had to continue with only fourteen players. Also at half-time you were not allowed off the field of play and there could be no advice or input from the coach or other players. Every match we appointed one of the touring party not selected to play to be the linesman for the match. Every match we had one of our players running the line as a match official, including test matches.

Fred Boshier was one of the journalists travelling with the All Blacks in 1960. Here are his comments about the thirteenth game of the tour.

It Happened on the Thirteenth[9]

> There must be something in superstition after all. The 13th match of the All Blacks' tour, played at Port Elizabeth on July 13, was also the most unsightly up to that stage. It was won by 13 points and, as the captain of the day, MacEwan, put it during the subsequent exchange of pleasantries, was won in the 13th round. As a further indication of the course the match took, one of the All Blacks said to me afterwards, 'You should have seen our dressing room. It was like a casualty clearing station.'

---

9   Boshier, F. W. (1960). *All Blacks in South Africa* (pp. 68–69). Wellington, NZ: Blundell Brothers.

From which it may be gathered that this was a match with some unusual features—but perhaps not quite as unusual as one might wish at times. It included much more than the normal amount of fighting, the exchanges of blows sometimes occurring in full view of everyone present.

The All Blacks never pretended to be anything that they were not and whenever they encountered provocative opponents, especially if the referee was slow to exercise control, they were liable to get away from orthodox Rugby. There were many matches from Test level down, however, which proved that the tourists were primarily interested in playing the game according to the Rugby code.

At least during the first half of the itinerary the fighting was limited to the matches against Boland and Northern Transvaal (in each of which they encountered front row forwards who had been in the 1956 Springbok team), and Eastern Province. There was, in fact, something in common between Northern Transvaal and Eastern Province—both were proud, rather than shamefaced about their "ruggedness." The Province captain; Allen, as much as said after the game that that was his team's style of play.

When the dispensing of justice on the Rugby field is done in the style of the vigilantes of frontier days it is logical to ask what has happened to the appointed authority. The question was pertinent in this instance. Mr. Carlson, the referee, was unusually light with his whistle in the first spell. The All Blacks had the rare experience of being able to play for appreciable periods without hearing the whistle. Unfortunately, things were going on which should have been dealt with promptly and sternly; and when the referee failed to intervene the players increasingly took matters into their own hands.

The first trouble spot was in the front row, with the New Zealand loose head side as the focal point. Packing as the tight head for Eastern Province was Holton, one of three brothers who achieved prominence as front row forwards. Holton was reputed to possess strength rivalling that of "Muscles" du Toit, while his method of packing was modelled on that of Amos du Ploy [sic], a 1955 Springbok of whom the All Blacks saw (and enjoyed) quite a lot while they were in Port Elizabeth. His tactic consisted of boring in on the hooker at an angle and thereby restricting his opportunities to heel the ball.

Packing against Holton was Anderson, one of the All Black forwards too often regarded as excess cargo and capable of giving the team excellent service whenever called upon. A heavily-built man, he would have thrived on hard work and it was only natural that he should find it difficult to preserve match fitness when required for only one match in four. However, as the man to cope with Holton, Anderson was about as good as any the All Blacks could field. When Holton tried to butt in on Boon, Anderson used his head (literally) to protect his hooker and when both he and Holton began to suffer recurring headaches after playing at being rams, he was ready to meet the Province man in the exchanges which inevitably followed.

How it came about that the referee failed to pick what was going on and deal with it accordingly was one of the mysteries of the match, since the effect upon the scrummaging was there for all to see. Whenever the forwards packed down with New Zealand having the loose head, the scrum would career away from the half-back like a crab heading back to the water. This happened not once but many times, yet all the referee did was to summon the perspiring, short-tempered forwards back to the original mark. After a while arms began to swing, attitudes became menacing and the middle of the scrum was a veritable powder keg. Still the referee did nothing about it, except to break up the forwards and speak to them. In the second half he must have decided that the All Blacks were to blame, since he penalised them in a number of scrums.

From the scrummage the trouble soon spread to other departments—if it was not there already. There was the sight of Horsley being held back with the ball nowhere near. Fortunately for him, as he attempted to beat off the obstructionist, the referee picked the right culprit and awarded New Zealand a penalty. Later, however, when Horsley (who worked like a champion all the way) was trying to shake an encumbrance off his leg the referee penalised him for a change Not long after this play was interrupted briefly while Horsley received attention to a gashed eyebrow. Boon was another who required the ministrations of the ambulance officials.

As was the case wherever the All Blacks went, attempts were made to persuade them when they reached the "Friendly City" of Port Elizabeth that the home team would be a pushover.

Eastern Province earlier in the season had been well beaten by Transvaal but had then readjusted their team with beneficial effects. A win over Boland had indicated that they were not to be taken lightly. The Province was proud of its record against overseas teams. In 1938 it was beaten only 6–5 by Sam Walker's British team; in 1949 the All Blacks won 6–3; in 1953 the Wallabies came home 16–9 but were said to merit a rather smaller margin; in 1955 Eastern Province beat the Lions 20–0.

Included in the team to play the All Blacks was Ulyate who, on the 1956 tour of New Zealand, had impressed his hosts after one of the finest strategic kickers they had seen. Ulyate went to Canada soon after 1956, returning last April. For some months he had been working on a sheep station of 6000 morgen (over 12,000 acres) about 350 miles from Port Elizabeth.

Ulyate was chosen as the full-back though still playing his club football at fly half. In the latter position was Wentzel, whom the All Blacks had just met at Durban as full-back for the Junior Springboks. The captain of the Eastern Province team was Allen, captain of the Junior Springboks in Argentina a year earlier. Holton and Allen both played against Scotland this year, while Griesel and Johnson were forwards of considerable experience.

The fact that Wentzel and Ulyate could both play at fullback or fly half suggested a leaning towards the kicking game. The suggestion was due to be fully substantiated and the reluctance of the home side to play the handling game had to be taken into account when criticism was later voiced at the lack of attractive play.

THIS match marked the first of two appearances by the Blacks at Boet Erasmus Stadium, which has replaced the much better known Crusaders' ground as the Rugby headquarters of Port Elizabeth. Named after a Province Rugby notability (Boet is an affectionate diminutive for "brother"), the stadium has an immense covered stand, is capable of seating 30,000 spectators and has a springy turf surface.

MacEwan won the toss and opened up facing the sun with the light breeze behind his team. Wentzel, kicking off, put the ball out on the full. A nice take by Ulyate while on the run alleviated the early minutes during which the teams mainly exchanged kicks. Pickering and MacEwan linked in a forward drive but the latter's pass fell clear. Then Allen chased a loose ball which he secured and fed to his backs only to see them fumble. Caulton shot through to the five-eighths sector and passed to Conway but the latter was blocked. A scuffle in front row proved a shadow of what was coming.

Play had been in progress 24 minutes when Truter speculated while under pressure. The ball went infield and a defender who took it was crash-tackled by Conway. The ball by this time was a red-hot rivet and when van Deventer got it he unloaded to Ulyate. Ulyate tried to kick clear but the ball was bustled in goal, where Truter, Singleton, and McMullen tried to collect it. They all missed out and Pickering fell on it for a try. D. B. Clarke failed to convert. 3–0. Five minutes later Clarke kicked a penalty goal from the 25, 15 yards in from touch. Wentzel beat A. H. Clarke rather badly before making a good run and then McMullen found a gap at five-eighth only to drop his pass at Lineen's toes. At half-time New Zealand led 6–0.

Near the end of the first spell Wentzel was injured and changed places with Ulyate. However, he was still fit enough to dropkick a beautiful penalty goal from 45 yards four minutes after the resumption. 6–3. Boon was in a sorry condition for a minute or so, but carried on. Lineen and Conway were seen in a loose rush. Ulyate threatened to kick his boot off and when an opponent illegally attached himself to Horsley, incurring an unpopular penalty, D. B. Clarke missed another 50-yard shot. Schonken was the next casualty of the vigorous milling. After 10 minutes' play the ball came from A. H. Clarke out to McMullen, who stepped inside Truter and passed to Lineen, who forced his way across. D. B. Clarke converted. 11–3. Another five minutes of mixed football went by and then an attack by the All Black backs finished with Caulton being blocked right on the line. Conway was on hand to grab the ball and score. D. B. Clarke's conversion made it 16–3.

More than half the spell remained but it was unproductive of scoring. Ulyate, dropkicking, missed an easy opportunity to give Eastern Province a penalty goal. Van Deventer almost broke his neck when he ran head-first into an All Black phalanx. Wentzel missed another dropkick from a penalty on the 25 and soon afterwards the referee called the captains together because of continued fighting among the forwards. MacEwan and Allen shook hands but it looked suspiciously like the fingertip touch of the boxing ring. After further pleasantries the game ended.

The outcome of the match stood to the credit of those who feel—and they do not belong to any particular union or country—that almost any measures are legitimate to win a Rugby match. Eastern Province, by a policy of "rugged" play allied to excessive kicking, sought to throw the All Blacks out of gear that they might be beaten or at least restricted to a low score. Because the All Blacks themselves were not working particularly well immediately behind the scrum the tactics achieved at least part of their purpose. As a result, even expatriated New Zealanders at the match were disappointed with the All Blacks' performance.

Players who did best for the tourists were D. B. Clarke, making a welcome return to form at full-back, and the little used forwards Pickering, Anderson, and Gillespie. The hardest toiler in the pack was Horsley, but MacEwan's part was most important. Urbahn and A. H. Clarke kicked too much with the latter again running sideways.

In the home team Ulyate's kicking may have detracted from the attractiveness of the game but it was long and accurate. Singleton played well at scrum half. Moorcroft was the outstanding forward, Johnson was active in the loose and Allen and Griesel worked hard.[10]

The last test of the tour of South Africa in 1960 was very similar in many respects to my first test in Wellington in 1956. The weather was windy, wrong selections were made by our selectors, and the score and results were identical.

---

10 See Appendix C 3 for match details.

When management announced the players, it was obvious to senior members of the touring team, that vital players in outstanding form had been omitted. A reshuffle of the backline was necessary given the unavailability of Terry Lineen through injury. But dropping Steve Nesbit and replacing him with Tony Davies at first five-eighth was foolhardy and without any logic. Dropping John Graham, the greatest thinker in the game and a really informed player, was a surprise not only to the team, but also to our supporters and the New Zealand press. I will always believe that if Steve Nesbit had been selected at first five-eighth, John Graham at number 8, Russell Watt moved from wing to centre, and Ralph Caulton and Frank McMullen selected as the wings; the result of the test match would have been a victory for New Zealand. The team we selected and the game plan we chose to play was too predictable and very easily countered by the opposition. And that was what happened as the game progressed. Steve Nesbit was a very competent and talented rugby player and his flair for the unpredictable always kept the opposition guessing what he was going to do next. That skill is something unique and we didn't have that in the backline that was selected.

In that era of rugby when a team was selected, the players always accepted without question the choices made by the selectors (the 'three wise men') and prepared accordingly for the task that lay ahead. That was certainly the case with the test at the famous Boet Erasmus stadium in Port Elizabeth.

The wind and sun were going to play a vital part in this game and we always played into the wind if we won the toss. But we lost the toss and Avril Malan elected to play into the wind and we had the kick-off. The crowd was estimated to be 59,000, the largest crowd for a game at the ground and Port Elizabeth was stretched to cater for all the visitors and some 2,000 were billeted in private homes, while others slept in cars. This was a big occasion and the test series was going to be decided on the result.

Right from the kick-off we went on attack. Very early in the game Don Clarke attempted a drop goal but it fell short and wide of the posts. It was very unlike Don 'The Boot' Clarke to fall short with a wind as strong as we were playing with. This attempt was followed by a missed try five minutes into the game. Frank McMullen picked up a loose ball and went to the blindside, dummied a pass then kept going totally confusing the defence; he was heading for a try when, out of the blue, Oxlee ankle-tapped him in a last-ditch attempt to stop a certain try. He wasn't held and in the same motion reached out and planted the ball over the scoreline. A certain try. We were horrified to see referee Burmeister award South Africa a penalty for a double movement. At this stage of the match the score could have been 8–0. We had lost two very important scoring opportunities. This was going to be the turning point of the game. Shortly after this Don Clarke kicked a penalty and we led 3–0. We were not using the elements to our advantage and we were making fundamental handling errors, which proved very costly. Halfway through the first half we were penalised and Lockyear kicked a great goal into the wind and at half-time it was all tied up 3–3.

In the second half Pelser scored a try by the posts, which was converted by Lockyear and South Africa led 8–3 which was the final score. In the closing minutes of the game, Don Clarke had to attempt to convert some rather difficult penalties but it wasn't his day. Pelser's try was scored from a pattern of play, which John Graham developed with the New Zealand forwards. That was the irony of this test match.

We had failed to capitalise on our scoring opportunities and, as a result, we lost the test and the series to South Africa. On the day we did not play well and South Africa fully deserved their win.[11]

Nevertheless the game was very significant for me and that is why I did not swap my jersey at the end of the game, which is often the custom. I wanted to keep this jersey as a memento because of the similarity between this game and my first test match for New Zealand in 1956. The jersey was eventually given to Joe Rooney and began its journey to Wales.

---

11 See Appendix C 4 for match details.

Two rugby writers, a South African and a New Zealander, sum up my contribution to the tour of South Africa.

> The All Black forwards, as the unit, were magnificent. In Nev MacEwan they had a lineout forward as good as any I have ever seen. His jumping was clear-cut and his hands were sure, while his scrum work was above reproach. Once or twice he showed extremely fine pace in the loose for a man of his size.[12]

> There may never have been a grander lock forward than the MacEwan of 1960. Of perfect physique for his position, he was an astonishing jumper for the ball in the line-outs, and a master man at retaining the ball once won. With fine calculation he would either feed the ball to his backs or forge through with almost unstoppable power. He could do everything required of him in the loose and was also a born leader.[13]

THE JERSEYS OF SIGNIFICANCE

There were a lot of similarities with my first test match and this game: the weather, the forward intensity, the standard of play, wrong players selected and the result. So the jersey was symbolic of all those memories and the events and so it was put away with the other two very significant jerseys. A Springbok jersey from 1956 and the British Lions Jersey from 1959.

---

12 Medworth, C. O. (1960). *Battle of the Giants*. Cape Town, SA: Howard Timmins.
13 Boshier, F. W. (1960). *All Blacks in South Africa*. Wellington, NZ: Blundell Brothers.

NEVEN MACEWAN

5. Travel Experiences and Work

Towards the end of 1956, after the Springbok tour, work offers with the oil companies were around and I was approached by an accountant to consider managing a service station, which required nothing else other than the rugby name. The salary they offered vastly exceeded that of a teacher. The lure of big money and the opportunity, in name only, to be my own boss was very appealing. The service station was the Ngaio Service Station and above the Awarua Street railway station I bought my first home, 14 Iwi Street, just 500 metres away. It was very close to work and was to become my first home with Jeannette Moulder after our marriage in 1957.

The decision to leave teaching and go into business was a bad decision. To operate a service station you need to be mechanically orientated and skilled in the engineering dynamics of motors. I had neither attributes; all I really knew was that water went into the radiator and petrol went into the petrol tank. Despite these limitations I went to work for the company. However, the company had an agenda that I was not aware of when I signed up. The real issue was that the oil company operating behind the scene wanted their products pushed, and wanted me to play my rugby for the Onslow Rugby Club purely from a business viewpoint. The company secretary overseeing the operation called to discuss these two issues two weeks after I had started the job. Europa Oil was expecting 60% of petrol sales. That was never going to be a possibility because there were five pumps covering every brand of petrol supplier, and we were serving up to four customers at a time. The previous owners had built their company up by providing personal service and selling the brand of petrol requested by their clients. The question of my leaving Athletic Rugby Football Club to play for Onslow was also raised but that was never going to happen. That bombshell brought about the end of my very short career as a service station manager.

I had been playing for the Athletic Rugby Football Club for three years and they had given me the opportunity of playing for the senior team. I had then been selected as a Wellington representative, and gained selection as an All Black. Shifting from Athletic was a no go. I resigned from the company and started to look for a new work opportunity.

Initially I went back to relieving as a schoolteacher and for a short time was teaching at Tawa Intermediate School. This temporary position lasted six months and during that period I was interviewed for a position with the shipping company Shaw Savill and Albion.

In August 1958 I took up a position with that company as a shipping clerk, working in the Inward Freight Department.

I really enjoyed the work at Shaw Savill and had experience in the Inward and Outward Freight Departments, working in close association with importers and exporters alike. I progressed through the departments and occasionally went with Malcolm Barnett, the personnel manager, to visit schools to talk about the company and to promote the company's image.

In 1962 I was appointed to canvass exporters and importers in order to obtain shipments of cargo for the fleet. My record of rugby achievements both for Wellington and the All Blacks helped me to get a foot in the door, especially with the wool buyers.

The company was very generous to me with time off to play representative rugby. I was never turned down when I applied for time to travel away with the Wellington Rugby Representative team, and it was always on full pay. On those occasions I always took time to visit the company's agents and offices around the country and I developed a network of contacts and support which was not only beneficial to my personal development but for Shaw Savill as well.

When I toured with the All Blacks to South Africa in 1960 and to Australia in 1962, I again took the opportunity to visit the company's offices and agents in those countries and developed my network of contacts worldwide. The support I had from the staff was helpful and inspiring and, when on the tour of South Africa, I sent regular recorded reports on the tour, which included interviews with team members, to the staff in the Wellington office.

As the selection of the 1963–64 team to UK and France neared, our general manager, Mr Harris, asked to see me. He told me that if I was selected for the tour he would like me to remain in England for a period of time and work in the company's head office in London once the tour was finished. That was an endorsement of the future he felt I had with the company. I was very excited at the prospect of working in London for a time. So in 1963 I really had something to work for, but a nagging injury which I developed on the 1960 tour of South Africa was going to become a serious issue needing surgery during the 1963 season. In addition I had a serious disagreement with the selectors that ended my All Black career.

My right knee would lock with the torn cartilage on occasions and, while it was very painful, when the leg was straightened it would free itself and settle down. I knew that each time my knee locked up it created further damage. But I just kept going. It was an attitude I had developed with the no-replacement rule for all international matches. As long as you could walk you kept going. Replacements in international matches didn't start until 1968 in South Africa in the series they played against the British and Irish Lions.

In 1963, in the international match at Athletic Park playing for Wellington against the touring England side, my leg locked up and I couldn't free it and had to be helped from the field. The troubled knee was no longer a secret—everyone knew about it and something had to be done. The medical team suggested that the cartilage was removed as soon as possible and a full recovery was assured. It would mean that I would be out for eight weeks but would be back subject to being selected for the final representative programme and the All Black trials. So the decision was made to go ahead with the operation immediately and then begin the rehab work needed to get back into the Wellington representative side. This meant I missed the opportunity that year of captaining Wellington in their triumphant Ranfurly Shield win over Auckland. That honour went to Mick Williment. It was a surprise win as everyone was expecting Auckland to win this match comfortably. However I was at the Wellington Railway Station on the Monday morning with Mayor Frank Kitts to welcome the victors home. Wellington then created history for the shortest tenure of holding the Shield, losing it the following Saturday to a well-drilled Taranaki side coached by JJ Stewart.

The operation on the knee went well and as soon as I came out of the anaesthetic I started in earnest to strengthen the thigh and leg muscles while keeping all aspects of my physical body as active as was practicable. I got fit for and played well in the All Black trials, but I learnt that I wasn't considered for the touring team by the selectors because of the comments I made to members of the selection panel when they picked their team to play England after the Wellington match. An additional factor was that the selectors obtained advice from my orthopaedic surgeon who stated he couldn't guarantee I wouldn't have recurring problems with my knee. But I am certain that it was my angry comments to the selectors in Wellington after we got beaten by England that really sealed my fate.

When the All Black team to play England on 25 May 1963 in Auckland was announced under the stand at Athletic Park my name was absent from the team. It was a big disappointment, but you take it on the chin and move forward to the next game and make sure that your efforts are of such a high standard that you cannot be overlooked. I learnt that approach when, after my first game for Wellington played against North Auckland in Whangarei, Clarrie Gibbons called me aside and told me that I had a great future in the game but that I would not be a regular member of the Wellington side this year. It was a very carefully presented statement to prepare me for the next team to be announced for Wellington in a few weeks' time. I knew that I had to go back to club football and produce outstanding performances to force the selectors to rethink their decision to drop me. I did just that and never lost my place when I was available to play for Wellington until I retired in 1967. I never expected selectors to explain their decisions when selecting a team. I believed they picked the best side on form to represent New Zealand.

On Saturday 18 May 1963, just after the team had been announced, I happened to walk into Neil McPhail coming out of the selectors' room and, by way of a comment, he said to me, 'Bad luck, Nev.'

I replied, 'It's not bad luck. You have picked your best side and next time, in terms of my performances, I will make it difficult for you to leave me out.'

Neil's reply incensed me. He stated, 'We don't know if it is our best side.' He indicated he was outvoted on my selection. My opinion of Neil McPhail went out the back door and my confidence in his ability to handle the reins of national coach diminished.

Later that same evening Bush and George, the other selectors, came into the bar where the members of the Wellington team were having a social gathering and a few beers. I had brooded on the selectors' decision to leave me out of the team and confronted Bush and George with my disappointment in being omitted by their decision. I should have kept my mouth shut and just kept my feelings to myself. But they copped a fair earful, questioning their parenthood and their qualifications to be selectors. I knew that from that point on I would never be selected to play for the All Blacks again. That was hard to come to grips with, even when I was selected to play in trial matches knowing that I would not be chosen no matter how well I played. Rugby Union officials are a power unto themselves and they certainly don't like being told by players that they are wrong.

So when I missed selection to tour the United Kingdom in 1963–64 many people were surprised and the rugby reporters were left questioning the selection of the team.

I was also absent from a large percentage of Wellington's domestic season that year because of my knee injury which necessitated a lengthy lay-off. As a consequence, I missed being part of the Wellington team that set a record, enduring to this day, for the shortest Ranfurly Shield tenure. It was on 31 August that Wellington, with their forwards—minus me—in magnificent form, took out an 8–3 win over Auckland to end that union's 25-match sequence of wins. Captain on that occasion was Mick Williment, who carried the Shield down Platform 9 at Wellington Station to the cheers of a large crowd that had gathered to meet the team on their return home on the Sunday. I was not overlooked though. The Post report of the occasion recorded that 'there were cries of "Where's Nev MacEwan?", as the crowd demanded the appearance of Wellington captain IN MacEwan, who is recovering from a knee operation. He was given a great cheer.'

I hadn't been in Auckland with the members of the side who were fit to play. The Wellington union had decided they were not justified in sending their injured captain as a spectator, and political sensitivities caused me not to accept any of the numerous offers I received from the public who wanted to take me anyway. So, like the rest of the crowd, I had just gone along to meet the train.

Among the crowd was the mayor, Mr FJ Kitts, whose message to the players was succinct. A paraphrase of it would read something like, 'Good to see the Shield here. Make sure you keep it!' It was not to be. Exactly one week after winning the shield, Wellington went out to defend it against a single-minded Taranaki team that included a certain KC Briscoe at halfback. Taranaki scored a try in the first minute and another one in the last minute; Wellington produced very little between the two tries, and succumbed to a loss of 17–3. Exit Ranfurly Shield.

My knee kept me out of this encounter too—though this time I was at the park!—but I was back in time to be named for the trials for the British tour. In the first matches I was named captain of the Possibles team for the early game. My effort to gain selection was probably not helped when my team lost 11–24, though it may not have been hurt when Stan Meads injured his back in a prematch practice and was forced to withdraw.

On the Saturday I was named—with Stan Meads—in the 3.00 pm game, from which the bulk of successful triallists traditionally come. Ron Horsley and Allan Stewart lined out against me.

I did not enjoy trial matches. For one thing, players competed against people, sometimes from their own team or district, who knew them and their play backwards. This was especially true as one's own career advanced on the international scene. Such people became very difficult to play against. It was hard to shine. Everybody was bent on being the one who shone and, if a player made a break, he wanted to do it all. There was no emphasis on being part of a team, and I regarded myself as a team man, not as an individualist. I concede that trial games have a place, especially as an arena where selectors can see how young players perform in higher company. But as games to play in, I rank them as a non-event; I can't recall a single score, or even whether I personally scored. I had one or two very good trial matches but it really depended on the selection of the teams that you were chosen to play in.

I did not produce my best in those trials, although I thought I had done enough to show the selectors that I had recovered completely from the cartilage operation. After the Wednesday game, the reporter present remarked that Ron Horsley and Kevin Barry had entered tour calculations. Of Nev MacEwan, it was observed that he was making a 'fighting comeback after a serious knee operation, and was understandably slow, but played out the full 80 minutes.' Before the Saturday match, my situation—which paralleled that of another couple of players—sparked a newspaper discussion on the exact role of trial matches. Fred Boshier, sports editor of Wellington's *The Evening Post*, wrote:

> Although MacEwan is a veteran of 20 internationals, and one of the greats on the 1960 tour of South Africa, he obviously cannot show his real ability in these trials. Can the selectors afford to leave him out because of that? It is not likely they will allow their final choice to be sabotaged by either an unpredictable trial incident or by such circumstances as have beset MacEwan, ST Meads and BT Thomas.

They could. They did. When the team was announced at twenty past six on the Saturday evening, MacEwan—and Thomas—were out, although ST Meads was in. Kevin Briscoe, named as vice-captain, stated his view as follows:

> I'm not aware of any suggestion of grog as a factor. If it was, it was well covered up—very well. It's hard to cover these things up on a rugby tour. There's usually one or two loose ends floating around. Journalists get into it too. But I thought Nev was a shock omission. He was a magnificent line-out forward, and he didn't play poorly. There was just this great big gasp when he wasn't selected. They couldn't understand. Once the team was away, though, there was no discussion on why he wasn't in. During the course of the tour I never found out why.

The answer probably lay in my knee operation, and in the form of my competitors. The comment from *The Evening Post* was that:

> Horsley played his way in with a series of splendid performances in the trials and throughout the season. The choice of locks and line-out specialists was not extremely difficult when the form of IN MacEwan was affected by a recent knee operation and Horsley revealed he knew all the answers. The Meads brothers and AJ Stewart were an outstanding trio throughout the trials.

The same newspaper delivered the final comment on my form a week or two later following Wellington's late-season game against Canterbury when it reported; 'MacEwan has not regained top form after his recent operation.'

So my thoughts of an All Black tour to Britain were laid aside. This looked like being even more disappointing than it would normally have been, because Shaw Savill had decided that if I made the team they would station me in London for a year on their behalf. Jeannette recalls,

> We were really looking forward to this, but then he didn't make the side—it was a big shock. It was made worse by one of the selectors coming up to him and saying, 'I voted for you, Nev.'
>
> Nev said, 'It's immaterial to me. You've chosen your best side.' The answer he got suggested a doubt as to whether they had, and something snapped in Nev then; he gave the selector a piece of his mind. I can't remember the words he used, but he was angry, and he'd been drinking, too, by this time. I guess that really cooked his goose—you don't go round telling off selectors. I don't think he was ever really considered again. Later he came back to play better rugby than he'd ever played. Athletic won the Jubilee Cup in 1965.

After the All Black team was named and I missed selection I thought my time in London with Shaw Savill would be over as well and I had resigned myself to that outcome. On the Monday morning life returned to some normality and I went off to work as usual. Half way through the morning I was summoned to the general manager's office and, after exchanging comments about the trial matches and the team selection, he said, 'Well Neven, we still would like you and Jeannette to go to London sailing on the *Northern Star* leaving Wellington in December.' Well I did everything to conceal my excitement and asked if I could have time to discuss this with Jeannette as we had our two boys, Doug and Bruce, to think about. We needed to consider what was best for them. That was going to be a big decision and one that was hard for both of us but particularly for Jeannette. I asked Mr Harris, if it would be acceptable to him to let him know our decision by Wednesday. He agreed and then the discussion started about our children. Would we take them with us or leave them at home? Where could we place them if we left them behind? Who would be best to look after them? Could we manage not being with them for six months? What about Doug starting school while we were away; did we really want to miss that very special day? We had some hard questions to answer and we needed to consider what was best for the children if we decided to go to London on our own. We had two days to come up with an answer.

The children were four and two years old and we didn't think taking them into an English winter would be wise. So the first decision we made was to leave them at home. Nelson, close to Jeannette's parents, felt ideal for us and when my brother Bill's wife, Margaret, offered to have the boys on the farm at Sherry River in Nelson, our questions were all answered. The decision-making process had been emotionally draining but there was nothing now to stop our time in London. We told Mr Harris that we would love to take up the company's offer to travel to London and that the children would remain in New Zealand. We planned to let our home in Seatoun while we were away as we had done in 1960 when I was away in South Africa. Jeannette (Nettie) had taken Doug back to Nelson and stayed with her parents. Once we had everything sorted out, the bombshell fell. Nettie told me four weeks later that she was pregnant and it had been confirmed by our doctor. The next day I made an appointment to see Mr Harris and I informed him of Jeannette's pregnancy and that I understood this could complicate the decision to go to London. He told me to leave the matter with him and he would let me know the company's decision after communicating with London and the ship's doctor. Well the Shaw Savill management decided that they wanted us to go and that the ship's doctor could look after Jeannette and any medical needs arising while travelling. We were off to spend six months in London!

We both missed the boys, but it would be fair to say Jeannette was more affected than I was, being pregnant, and she would be very emotional when she saw children and especially so on Christmas Day. When Jeannette got home, Bruce hardly knew her. He was calling Margaret 'Mummy Marget'. Jeannette remembers that we saw

The Sound of Music while we were away. It was full of cute little kids, and quite the worst kind of therapy for her in those surroundings.

But we did get to the most amazing places in London. I played that season for the Blackheath Rugby Club, which had some very interesting people among its members. We were invited to dinner once, just the two of us, by the Queen's orthopaedic surgeon. His wife was an editor of *Vogue*. That was really quite something. We met some fabulous people, and did some wonderful things.

When we arrived in England, someone from the press met us at the ship, and there was a headline: 'MacEwan Arrives'. Jeannette couldn't believe it. She thought it was because of the current All Black team on tour.

Jeannette's surprise at being met at the ship by the press prompts the question: Did the rugby publicity get to her as a wife? Or, a wider question: Did she find it frustrating or demeaning, being a 'Mrs All Black' with even the gynaecologist wanting to talk rugby all the time?

Jeannette believed it was her responsibility to support me in what I did; after all, I had made it to the top in my rugby and this had opened doors of opportunity in the workplace. But there were silly things Jeannette found harder to deal with. For example, one press photographer wanted a photograph of Jeannette in the maternity home knitting an enormous sock!

Jeannette got used to people recognising her only when she was with me. However, she did remember one day especially when the American ambassador, John Henning, met her in the street and said, 'Hello Mrs MacEwan.' It blew her away because he was the first dignitary who remembered her on her own. But I suppose that's an ambassador's job—remembering people and making them feel special.

There were some great experiences because of the rugby. We got to all sorts of places. Not many people get to go to a ball at Grosvenor House, especially not pregnant ones. It was after the England versus Ireland test match. The men all went to a reception, and the girls met at Grosvenor House. Jeannette went with a doctor of some rank, who drove a limousine and took inordinate care of his pregnant guest: he had her belted in, in a complete harness, and she could hardly move. The great care didn't actually stop him from calling in at various pubs on the way, but Jeannette couldn't get out. She was imprisoned in the limousine. Then, when I arrived at Grosvenor House, Jeannette was dancing with Lord somebody or other who was nearly as big around as she was. They were dancing at arm's length away from each other.

There was a continuous supper at that ball—a most lavish spread. Jeannette and I had never been to a ball with a continuous supper before. Jeannette had bought a special evening dress for the occasion, because it really was a very special event. But evening dresses were short at that time, and there was Jeannette with this lace thing on, hem above her knees, and dancing at arm's length with her partners.

England v Ireland match at Twickenham

Jeannette remembers the England V Ireland match well but not for the result or the game.

> We went to the England v Ireland game at Twichenham and after the match Neven went with Tony O'Reilly(the great Irish winger who toured New Zealand in 1959 with the British Lions) to the dressing rooms and I was waiting for him to escort me to the bar when I was accosted by a Rugby Union official. I was holding a rug from the Mosgiel Woollen Mills that Nev had been given in 1959— they'd given one to each of the players in the Lions team, and also to the All Blacks. They had a fern leaf on them, and a Lions' badge, and each player's initials. Ours had 'N. MacE'. Well, I was standing there at Twickenham, not far from the official box, when this official approached me and said, 'Madam, is that your rug?' 'Yes,' I said. 'It's got my husband's initials on it.' It turned out that the NZRFU had given twenty-four of these rugs to the official box at Twickenham, and he thought I'd pinched one. He was most apologetic.

I had my own comment on the 1963–64 team, the team I had such fond hopes of making. It was a very good side, and I was warmly received when I made contact with the members I knew in the team. Yet, in another way, it was almost better not to be there—I felt so much out of it. Jeannette and I flew to Edinburgh to see the Scottish test, and on the flight we were seated with Andrew Mulligan, the halfback for the British Lions in 1959, and he asked me what I thought the outcome of the test match would be. I forecasted problems. It was a crucial stage of the tour, that vulnerable stage—over half way, but the end not yet in sight, and you have to tough it out. The team had been very successful, just the one narrow loss, yet I remember saying that they'd do well to get a draw in the test. Famous last words! The All Blacks drew with Scotland nil all.

JEANNETTE REMEMBERS THAT DAY

> We went to see the Scottish test, the nil all draw. It was a cold day, and the field was frosty all around the edges, but playable on the pitch because of the 'electric blanket'. A brewery had donated an under-the-surface electrical blanket to thaw out the ground in frozen conditions. We don't think of those sorts of things here in New Zealand.

The team went from strength to strength in the later stages of the tour, and then came the wonderful finale in the Barbarians' match in Cardiff. Jeannette and I were again in attendance, with the expectant Jeannette in the grandstand; I was on the terraces among the Welsh supporters. It was incredible to be there, among the Welsh people. When Whineray scored the final try and the crowd just suddenly burst into song, I was simply proud to be a New Zealander. There were tears in my eyes. It was one of my most moving rugby experiences, and I wasn't even playing.

Ian Clarke was playing for the Barbarians that day and later I was invited to play for the Barbarians in their annual fixture against East Midlands playing in the Mobbs Memorial match. I was also invited to be a member of their Easter tour of Wales, but I turned it down.

Hard decision? Not really; I'd promised Nettie we'd tour Scotland over Easter. Jeannette has her own memory of the Barbarians' match:

> It's the other moment from the game that all New Zealanders remember—Ian Clarke's goal from a mark. People like Nev say they'd seen him kick and they weren't surprised, but ask yourself. He had no points on the tour, certainly no goals, definitely not from marks, and neither did anyone else, not even his famous goal-kicking brother, Don. The score was close at the time, but when it finished at 36–3, all the points had been scored by New Zealanders. Anyway, when he stepped up and kicked the goal, and looked so smooth about it, I screamed so loudly up in the stand, that two Welshmen in front of me looked around and said, 'Eh, lass, it's not the Beatles!'

I got around a fair bit. It wasn't a holiday; I had to see the other side of the shipping business, what happened at the London end to business I'd conducted in New Zealand. I worked in the Inward Freight department of the London Office, and on the docks where I saw Shaw Savill's goods unloaded and redirected to markets. I spent a lot of time with importers and exporters while in London, and then travelled to woollen mills in Lancashire and other places as part of my brief to get to understand all aspects of the shipping trade. I had time to see shipping operations around England and the Continent. I visited Southampton and Hull and, having joined the ship's crew on the *Coptic*, visited Dunkirk, Antwerp, Bremerhaven and Hamburg. I was able to see ports at work, and to observe developments and trends.

After that trip, I could see that the future of shipping was limited in its then-current form. I suggested the future of the travel industry was tour groups by air, especially sports tours, and Shaw Savill picked that up. I had the ideas, but the practicalities of getting everything together was a different kettle of fish. Other people also commented that I should have been used in an 'ideas' capacity, but not allowed near the business management. This was very similar to Dad so many years before.

INTERESTING EXPERIENCES

I got a better idea of balance about rugby from the Blackheath club. It's often been said that New Zealanders get fit to play rugby, while the English play rugby to get fit. There seemed to be some truth in that comment. In New Zealand before a rugby game I would have a light meal at least three hours before kick-off and it normally consisted of a steak and salad. I would then turn up at the venue at least one hour before kick-off. My first match for Blackheath at Rectory Field was totally different. Two club officials invited me out to lunch and the lunch consisted of a four-course meal plus liquid refreshments. At the conclusion of the meal it was a hurried trip to the Rectory Field arriving 10 minutes before kick-off. I must admit that I didn't feel like playing a game of rugby. The soup, entree, main course and pudding plus the sherries, wines and liqueurs had all affected my preparation for the game. On top of all this I met the team for the first time and I was made captain for the day. Jeannette took her place in the clubhouse on the first floor above the changing rooms; it had ceiling-to-floor glass windows, a roaring fire at one end of the room and a waiter to serve drink requests. Despite my lack of preparation for the game I made a reasonable contribution and Blackheath won.

I was surprised at one aspect of English rugby: bowler-hatted English gentlemen who, at the after-match functions, and influenced by far too much alcohol, behaved abominably and did things to outrage the most beery of New Zealand rugby heavies.

So our time in England was full, right up until we came home. Jeannette had to come home earlier than me. Although Shaw Savill management had insisted the ship's doctor could mind Jeannette on the way over, the authorities wouldn't allow her on the boat on the way back. The doctors claimed we had got the dates wrong, and they weren't prepared to risk having Jeannette on board the *Northern Star*, so she had to fly. Non-stop, by Comet! I came home by sea as scheduled, and arrived in time for the birth of our third son, Angus. He was named after the captain of the *Northern Star*, Angus Baber. We did have our dates right! His birth no doubt caused Dr Findlay great pleasure in producing another rugby player of the future. I arrived home just after the start of the New Zealand rugby season; I had been in training all the way home by running around the promenade deck every morning before breakfast. I started playing club football almost immediately on arriving home, and for Wellington, and I had a very good season back playing great rugby and really enjoying the challenges.

Jeannette would not claim to be any judge of a rugby player's form, and insists she remained quite ignorant about most of it throughout my playing career. Her assessment of my play at this time, though, was shared by many, including the All Black captain, Wilson Whineray. He commented from the perspective of one who might know,

> I played against Nev two or three times round 1964. He was having a very good provincial season for Wellington. He had a couple of hell-of-a-good provincial seasons. He seemed to have found a new lease of life, not worrying about being in the All Blacks or not, but just playing good rugby. To play against him made you realise he was a really top performer again, really dynamic, playing well. He'd gone up, come down, got lost, missed Britain, and then he somehow reappeared, and he was outstanding. He had a hardness in his play, and an eagerness. He wasn't a reactive player, he was proactive, looking for the ball, and when he ran with it with a bit of energy he took some knocking over. He was a big beggar. And he really was outstanding again—in that form, I think in another season he would've probably pushed his way back into it. Certainly had he been a year or two younger. Age was starting to catch him up—he was on the wrong side of 30. He was a very good player, no question of it. And a lovely, gentle person.

I was genuinely enjoying my rugby at that stage. As Whineray speculated, I had felt free from the pressures of half-expecting All Black status, and I was able to simply play the game of the day, whether club or provincial. Athletic had an outstandingly good season in 1965, winning all their matches but one, and gaining the Jubilee Cup for the first time since 1945. I got as much satisfaction from that cup win as from anything else in rugby. Athletic went on to win the Jubilee Cup once more before the club's amalgamation with Onslow and Karori to form Western Suburbs in 1983.

The Jubilee Cup was the first of Athletic's two notable feats in the mid-1960s. The second, in 1966, was relevant to an amalgamation issue. It was a most ambitious world tour, the whole purpose of which was to attract young players to the club to offset the decline in playing numbers caused by increasing suburbanisation. As a central city club, Athletic was not the logical destiny of any local college, and they were getting only imports to Wellington to swell their ranks. The numbers in those ranks were slumping, and the club was losing incoming players to its rivals. They were losing their feeding ground. Ray Dellabarca, Bob McCullough, Gary Watt, Theo Weyden and I mooted the tour idea, and it took place in October of 1966. The full story of the tour is documented in the book *Wellington Athletic Rugby Football Club World Tour 1966* written by myself with Seamus Coogan.[14]

I played through to 1967 with Athletic and Wellington, notching up my 200th first-class game in the process; I actually played my last game for the province in yet another fruitless Ranfurly Shield challenge.

I can still see it. We led Hawkes Bay 12–6 and there was not long to go; we had a grip on the game. Then they came back to 12–9. Then Mattie Blackburn went off, and our inside backs had to reshuffle. Finally, with no time left at all, Blair Furlong drop-kicked a goal and they sneaked out of it at 12–all. Blair had no right to kick that goal; it was a fluke, but I'm sure he won't recall it like that.

Wellington had lost a Shield match to Taranaki in 1964 by a dropped goal too, (3–0 that day); the goal was kicked by a replacement fullback from the Eltham club, Neil Paterson, standing in for the injured regular. With the game scoreless after 50 minutes, Paterson let go with a drop kick 'that he had no right trying for,' said Kevin Briscoe. 'It was miles too far away—out of his range.' Like Furlong, Paterson had only a hazy view of the rights of it. He just kicked the goal. Wellington failed both times.

---

14 Copies of this book are available through the website www.nevenmacewan.com.

My rugby-playing career, then, finished at the end of the 1967 season. It had brought opportunities and rewards exceeding those offered to most players. It had offered moments of delight and despair, of fame and frustration. It had brought injury and enjoyment. Its influence was to remain with me for years. Even today, I meet people who say to me, 'Are you the rugby man?' and there begins a conversation, which might otherwise be difficult to open. Rugby made a profound impact on my life.

But the world is not oval, and even All Blacks have to eat. Challenges in life have to be found and conquered. I worked for Shaw Savill for 10 years until I left them in 1967 in order to establish the travel firm of Nev MacEwan Travel with my old friend Mick Williment. We set the company up, but Williment was working for another company and it was deemed imprudent for his name to be used in the new venture. He was therefore a silent partner. When Mick left the cigarette company he was working for we changed the name to MacEwan Williment Travel until 1971 when it became Williment World Travel.

Mick and I had much in common; he also was unexpectedly dropped from the All Black team, which was to tour the British Isles in 1967. The rugby public was stunned. They were going there only because a proposed tour to South Africa had been called off when the hosts refused to approve the inclusion of Maori players and New Zealand refused to send a team without them. It was less than a month since Williment had played the last of his nine tests, and scored the last of his 70 points for New Zealand in the 75th Jubilee test against Australia at Athletic Park. Still, when the touring team was named, the sole fullback was the durable Fergie McCormick, who went on to enjoy a great tour. Williment's time was then spent establishing the new business.

One of the aims of the company was to facilitate travel by sports teams. I had been to England and Japan with the Athletic Club side, which was the first-ever world tour by a club side and I had anticipated the future of such tours, together with supporters' tours following

New Zealand sides. It seemed to both of us that we could provide a service and tap a market; being well-known sporting names would be an advantage. My experience with the Shaw Savill subsidiary company, White Heron Travel, was very helpful. The company was established and our very first tour was busloads of people travelling to the Bowl of Brooklands in New Plymouth to attend the concert by The Seekers. The number of people that joined that tour exceeded our wildest dreams. It was a very successful event and we should have concentrated solely on tours like that instead of trying to be accredited as a travel agent.

Our company had its ups and downs. It broke into some of the most competitive franchise fields and established new business, but it also fell victim to a gifted swindler who was numbered among its customers. As a direct consequence of the 'Urquhart affair' the company would eventually require a substantial capital injection to survive.

The company was bailed out by Chandris Lines, which wanted to move into the package tour business. They injected finance into MacEwan/Williment and kept the company afloat. They also injected a number of auditors who began to ask questions. As a consequence, I was summoned home from a tour I was escorting in the UK, and required to answer questions about the 'creative accountancy practices' I had used when trying to keep the company afloat. Some comments inferred that I had misappropriated funds, which I strongly denied.

The result of the meeting was that I signed all my rights, claims and shareholding in the company to the Chandris Shipping Line. I was then asked to leave the company. They were right: the company had to be saved for its future, and I had to accept the responsibility for the financial difficulties it was facing.

However, the travel company never recovered from the Urquhart affair. A farmers' tour to Calgary Stampede, which held so much potential for the future of our company, turned to custard. On the night the group was departing from Auckland, Dalgety Travel, who had issued travel tickets and vouchers for the tour, informed me they had not been paid. Despite assurances by Donald Urquhart that his bank had made the payment, Dalgety never received the funds. Donald was a very plausible man and his network was a who's who of Australia and around the world notoriety. He was based in Sydney and had exported products to Asia and had been marketing tours from Australia for people associated with the agricultural industry. He was in New Zealand to put this tour to Canada together. We offered him the facilities of our office in Willis Street while he was in New Zealand. That was the first error we made and later he asked Mick if he could be his tour leader. So by association we were identified with this farmer's tour to Canada. The tour was marketed both in Australia and New Zealand and the brochure promoting the tour had our company name on it along with Dalgety Travel. The ticketing company had received no money and we hadn't received a cent, so where was the money? Donald was already in Vancouver finalising arrangements and there was no way to speak to him. Mick was in the departure lounge at Auckland Airport waiting to board the aircraft and Dalgety Travel threatened to cancel the tour unless they had assurance from me that our company would pay them the next day.

I immediately rang our accountant and asked him what we should do. His advice was to tell Dalgety Travel, who were the wholesaler for the package tour, that we were in no way responsible for this debt and that there was no liability from our company to the members of the touring group. However, morally I felt we had to do something because we had been very cleverly promoted as supporting this tour. In a word we had been conned. Our accountant confirmed yet again that we were not liable for Urquhart's debts but the final decision was mine. The bill was substantial and, if paid, could cripple the fledgling company. The adverse publicity wouldn't have helped us either.

Mick and I couldn't win either way. The only way we had a slight chance to get the money back was for the tour to go ahead and for Mick to have Urquhart arrested in Vancouver on a charge of conspiracy to defraud, and then try to recover the money from Urquhart.

So I rang Mick and gave him the news that the tour could proceed and that, on arrival, he had to lodge a charge of conspiracy to defraud against Urquhart with the authorities and insist that he be held in custody. Urquhart was arrested and placed in custody. The next day Mick went to talk with Urquhart only to be informed that he had been released as he had put up a plausible case and the authorities could not hold him on the evidence Mick had documented and provided. Urquhart, once released from custody, simply disappeared. He took no part in the farm tour which was a great success, but our money had disappeared along with Urquhart. I found out later that he had flown from Vancouver to Tokyo charging the flight to Avery Brundage, head of the International Olympic Committee at that time. Urquhart's wife and daughter left New Zealand on the same day and we were never able to find any trace of where they went or even if they went together.

I worked in a variety of jobs after leaving the travel company. I worked as a dustman, aircraft loader for Air New Zealand at Wellington Airport, cleaning sections and houses of rubbish, and writing a travel information page for *The Dominion*. I was then introduced to 'Golden Products' a pyramid-selling scheme offering a range of biodegradable cleaning products.

PALMERSTON NORTH

I was looking for a work opportunity to suit my skills and ability and in 1971 applied for the position of Public Relations Officer for Palmerston North.[15] The employer was the Palmerston North Public Relations Organisation. I was invited to an interview that was held on a Saturday and at the end of the day was offered the position which I accepted. My role began in January 1972.

My job was to promote the city and the area and to highlight what could be achieved in Palmerston North in order to bring people to the city. We looked at all aspects of promoting the city and its surrounds. Palmerston North is centrally situated and ideal to cater for the

---

15 My CV is listed in Appendix A. It was prepared in 2003 when I applied for the All Black Manager's position in 2003–04.

growing convention business. It would require more accommodation and facilities. Not everyone was as keen as I was on these proposals. Local moteliers were not at all enthusiastic about this, despite the fact their occupancy rate was among the highest in New Zealand.

One of my responsibilities as the Public Relations Officer of Palmerston North City was to encourage new establishments. Developments over the next fifteen years were to vindicate this strategy. Massey University attracts many conferences, especially during the summer weeks. Massey also has a number of extramural students in attendance in May and August. We saw great potential in all of this. In addition, there's some pretty good fishing in the Manawatu rivers—though not everyone knows that—and, of course, Palmerston North is within a day's trip to visit Napier, Wanganui, New Plymouth, Taupo, Masterton, Wellington and the Tongariro National Park with its ski fields.

I found the job interesting and rewarding. My family happily settled into Palmerston North as well. Jeannette even got to look at the house before we bought it. The house in Church Street which we bought had a very humble kitchen, but it met more of our other needs than anywhere else. We were happy enough about it. Douglas, who'd had a year at Wellington College, moved quite naturally into Palmerston North Boys' High School, and Bruce and Angus followed him there in due course. Jeannie was later to attend Palmerston North Girls' High, and finish at Awatapu College.

Jeannette settled well into the new life in Palmerston North becoming associated with the children's school and sporting activities. She also became involved with the Palmerston North Operatic Society where she could express her exceptional musical talents; joined Palmerston North Toastmistress Club; and, with our two youngest children, Angus and Jeannie, became a member of All Saints church choir. I got involved with the Queen Elizabeth College Old Boys Rugby Football Club taking up the position of senior coach for three years. Also, John Sinclair, one of the founders of the New

Zealand Rugby Museum, invited me to serve on the committee, which I accepted and eventually became their chairman.

There were six momentous events I was associated with while in the position of Public Relations Officer:

- Rose Sunday, which was held in association with TV3. Its main attraction was Rob Guest who headed a grand list of entertainers for the day. The weather was beautiful and the event was attended by thousands of people from all over the lower half of the North Island.
- Two Telethons where Palmerston North functioned as one of the satellite centres around New Zealand.
- The Miss New Zealand Show in 1978, which was televised. It was a live show going out to all New Zealand fronted by Max Cryer and produced by our own Pat Snoxell.
- Lunch with the Queen and the Duke of Edinburgh when I was a city councillor.
- Promoting the inaugural flight of a Boeing 737 into Palmerston North.
- Playing the genie in the Christmas pantomime Aladdin.

I also hosted the Governor General Sir Denis Blundell at the official opening of the museum but this time in my role as chairman of the New Zealand Rugby Museum.

I always had good creative ideas but I needed to focus on that gift and be surrounded by others with the skills to complement me. I have learnt the secret to real life and it is contained in this quotation from the Bible:

> I have learned, in whatever state I am, to be content. I know what it is to be in need, and I know what it is to have more than enough. I have learned this secret, so that anywhere, at any time, I am content, whether I am full or hungry, whether I have too much or too little (Philippians 4:11–12).

Other notable activities included:

1974   I coordinated the fundraising activities for Palmerston North's contribution to the 1974 Commonwealth Games held in Christchurch.

1975–76   I organised the Ranfurly Shield parades for the city of Palmerston North. I developed the concept of Palmerston North being a conference venue for New Zealand and founded the Convention Centre Bureau.

1976–79   I was elected a City Councillor for Palmerston North and was appointed Chairman of the Economic Development Committee.

I held the position of Public Relations Officer until I resigned in 1978 and purchased and ran my own business, the Terrace End Book and Toy Shop.

The year 1979 saw my fall from a position of status to that of a criminal, the result of making wrong choices over the years and never believing that one day they would come back to bite me.

JAMES BALLANTYNE MACEWAN
CIRCA 1896

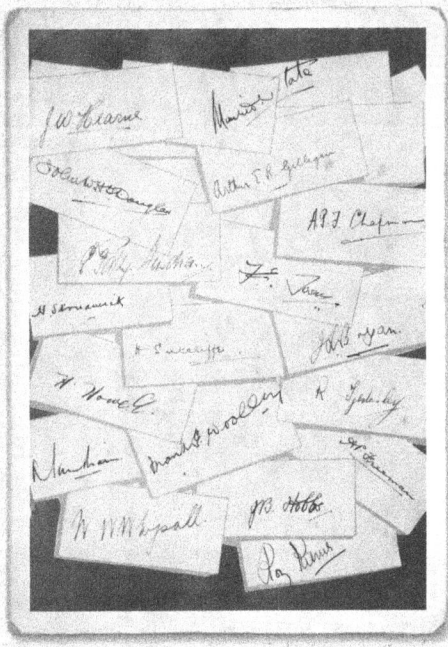

MCC TOURING SIDE
1924/25 AUTOGRAPHS

GRANNY KERR
AND MY MOTHER

MY GRANDMOTHER, MARY MACEWAN
WITH MY MOTHER
IVY HEATHER MACEWAN

THE HORSE-DRAWN CARAVAN WITH THE HORSE (JEAN) AND GIG

THE EVENING POST. FRIDAY, APRIL 11, 1930.

MACEWAN-KERR WEDDING

MACEWAN—KERR WEDDING.—A wedding which created much interest in Wellington yesterday was that of Ivy Heather, daughter of Mr. and Mrs. W. J. Kerr, of Carnoustie, Scotland, and Ian Arthur, only son of Mr. and Mrs. J. B. MacEwan, of Wellington. The bride and bridegroom leaving St. Paul's Pro-Cathedral after the ceremony.

Dad and his mother M E MacEwan (nee Fisher) on his wedding day

My birth place 1 St Vincent Avenue, Remuera, Auckland

Bill Pat and Neven at 1 St Vincent Ave, Remuera, Auckland

Brother Bill, Me and Brother Pat 1938

The Four Brothers Neven, Michael, Pat & Bill
with Granny Kerr at Richmond, Nelson

Nelson College Senior, 1952

NELSON COLLEGE 1ST XV 1952
I'M SITTING SECOND ROW 3RD FROM THE RIGHT

WADESTOWN SCHOOL TEACHER
1955

Ken McGregor (Australian Rules Player and Australian Tennis Champion) and Me, Jumping for the ball at Wadestown School 1955

1956 1st Test Jersey

Jeannette and Neven the day before their wedding in 1958, Winton, Southland.

My two soccer players Bruce (left) and Doug at the Basin Reserve, Wellington playing for Seatoun

Training on the deck of the *Northern Star* Cape Town 1964, on my way home after working in Head Office, London for Shaw Savill and Albion Co Ltd 1963/64

'Athletic Rugby Football Club Wellington 1966 World Tour' This book is available from the New Zealand Rugby Museum and from nevenmacewan.com

Me and our van after the accident

The people involved with the return of my 4th Test 1960 All Black Jersey. Jan Maruska, Lynley MacEwan, Angus and Donald Stott.

Me with Roddy Evans and his son Bas at Cilfynydd, Wales 2005

Joe Rooney presenting me with Roddy Evans's 1959 3rd Test Jersey

Jeannette MacEwan, known as Net

The MacEwan Clan, 2014

Angus and Lynley MacEwan, Bruce and Rachel MacEwan, Neven and Jeannette, Moira and Doug MacEwan, Jeannie and Greg Fayerman

Photo: Ross Land

Neven MacEwan All Black number 578 is capped by NZRU President John Sturgeon during the New Zealand All Blacks Test Capping Ceremony at Westpac Stadium. June 2009, Wellington, New Zealand.

ME AND THE PORTRAIT
PAINTED BY JULIA LYNCH IN 1959

PHOTO: NEW ZEALAND RUGBY MUSEUM INC.

THE 1956 NEW ZEALAND TEAM VS SOUTH AFRICA AT WELLINGTON.
NEVEN SECOND ROW 5TH FROM THE LEFT.

ALL BLACKS THIRD TEST TEAM VS BRITISH ISLES, LANCASTER PARK
AUGUST 29, 1959. ALL BLACKS 22, BRITISH ISLES 8.
NEVEN BACK ROW, 4TH FROM THE LEFT.

NEW ZEALAND RUGBY REPRESENTATIVES, SOUTH AFRICAN TOUR 1960.
NEVEN SECOND ROW, 6TH FROM THE LEFT.

Old mates. Neven with Kevin Skinner.

The return of the jersey

6. The Tale of the Jerseys Concludes

This chapter details how I reclaimed some of my famous rugby jerseys. Before I continue, it is hard to express the fullness of my admiration for the people of Wales. Don Hayward, as you have read, was a close friend and mentor; Roddy Evans was an incredible adversary; while it was Joe Rooney who reunited me with Roddy and my jerseys. Thanks to the efforts of my son, Angus, you will see how I deepened my bond with the Welsh, in particular the rugby club and town of Cilfynydd, and reclaimed an important part of my heritage. In Appendix B1 you will find further information on Joe Rooney and, in Appendix B2, correspondence between Angus, myself, and Nigel Jones.

JOE ROONEY
Joe and I first met in the late 1960s along with Mick Williment. We visited Turangi as guests of the Pihanga Rugby Football Club to take the senior team's practice and share at a sportsmen's function in the evening. It was a great weekend and the hospitality was superb.

In 1974 Joe was invited by College Old Boys RFC, Palmerston North, to attend an end-of-year function, along with the late Jim Heaphy, the late John (Flea) Fleury and his brother Bill, and Alan New. I was MC for the night, and the boys from Pihanga Rugby Club were all invited back to my home after the function. Joe later asked me if I would give him an All Black rugby jersey for a club back in Wales to encourage the ties with his old friend Cyril Mahoney, and cement ties between the Welsh people and New Zealanders. I gave Joe three international rugby jerseys: a South African jersey from the 1956 tour of New Zealand, the one I exchanged with Basie Viviers the captain of the Springbok Team; a British Lions jersey that I exchanged with Roddy Evans during the 1959 tour of New Zealand; and the All Black jersey was the one I wore in 1960 in the last test against South Africa played in Port Elizabeth, South Africa.

Joe would be so inspired by later events he penned two beautiful poems that I have included in this chapter.

THE JERSEY

> This jersey and its history, the stories it could relay.
> And yet in careful storage, this football jersey lay
> It found its way across the seas and like the prodigal son
> It has returned from whence it came; yet its story is not done.
> It forged friendships many years ago—one that stands today.
> And if it could speak, and it will, what will that jersey say?
>
> 'I was worn by a warrior who played with passion and with pride;
> A true gladiator, there was no place to hide.
> He went into battle; gallant foes he would meet.
> When you don an All Black jersey, there is no retreat.'
>
> I speak of determination and kinship,
> The battles and triumphs of this enduring game;
> The friendship it has formed through the MacEwan name.
> The story has now been told, I'm back where it all began,
> with that proud warrior and the MacEwan family clan.

THE 'PRODIGAL' 1960 ALL BLACK JERSEY RETURNS HOME

The stories those three international rugby jerseys could tell would amaze you, but they attracted many New Zealanders and rugby-crazed Welsh people to visit Cilfynydd. Similarly, many Welsh people visited New Zealand as a result. Thus, Joe's vision to cement Welsh-New Zealand relationships through his association with the game of rugby and the three jerseys exceeded his wildest dreams. The means by which I was reacquainted with my All Black jersey definitely exceeded mine. The time was 10.00 pm on Wednesday 2 November 2005 (New Zealand time) when I began writing about the lead-up to my trip to Wales. What follows comes from those very notes, made on the flight.

Angus and I had been flying for six hours from Auckland to Kuala Lumpur, after which I had another 16 hours of flying ahead of me. We had a wonderful meal, and flying business class with Malaysian Airlines was indeed a luxury. Ironically, I had never flown anything other than economy in all my years of travel and working in the travel industry. After dinner, I watched the movie *Spiderman 2*; it was fun, nonsense. I then sat back and listened to my favourite music, and the song 'Just Show Me How To Love You' played in my earphone. Tears flowed down my face as I recalled what happened in the lead-up to my journey, and what this trip was really all about.

Earlier, in the day I had left Palmerston North with Air New Zealand to join Angus in Auckland. It was hard to see Nettie walking away and leaving me at the airport. She was off to her teaching commitments at Freyberg High School. I knew this trip was going to be an amazing experience, and I wanted her to share it. She has always been there for me, particularly in the time of hopelessness and despair. I knew for certain that I would miss her on this trip. But what was really behind this journey? Well it's all about the return of an All Black Rugby jersey, the one I wore in 1960 in the 4th test at Port Elizabeth in South Africa. The result of the test series depended on which team won the last match.

Just thinking about this fateful match that took place just over 45 years ago brought back many memories, joys and disappointments.

On 1 May 2005, my third son Angus phoned to wish me a happy birthday. This was all well and good, but then he followed up with what I thought was joke. Angus is a real practical joker and I thought he was pulling my leg. So I dismissed the comment without thinking much more about it. He told me he was taking me to Wales at the end of the year so I could be presented with one of my All Black playing jerseys and bring it home for the family to treasure in the years ahead.

Jeannette and I were having dinner with our daughter Jeannie and her husband Greg, so I went back to enjoy my dinner and told them Angus had rung to wish me happy birthday. I made no mention of his comments concerning a trip to Wales, as I felt it was a non-event. I had other issues on my mind. Angus had no idea Jeannette and I had decided I would retire from my position as chaplain at Manawatu Prison on 29 October 2005, a position I had held for 16 years. We had further decided that Jeannette would retire from her position as a teacher at Freyberg High School at the end of the same year.

Later on the same night I received a call from Angus's wife Lynley wishing me happy birthday. She added that their present was going to be something special, and Angus had already told me what it was. It was only then I realised Angus wasn't joking and that what had seemed like a joke was in fact a firm proposal. Nevertheless, I had some questions: What jersey was it? How did he find out about it? How on earth would he be able to have it returned to me after 38 years. I now told Jeannette and Jeannie about Angus and Lynley's gift. Their reactions and questions were the same as mine: as a group we were amused, bewildered, excited and more than a little anxious.

A month out from my retirement, Angus finally confirmed the dates of travel. So I found out we were departing New Zealand one week after my official retirement date. I still hadn't mentioned to Angus I was retiring; moreover, when writing back to Angus, I mentioned the whole adventure defied comprehension. Angus's reply (below) had me in tears, and brought back amazing memories of special events, and people who came along to assist and boost me at key moments in my life.

REPLY AND SUMMATION FROM ANGUS MACEWAN

Through the actions of Angus, I realised once again that God who had saved me in 1979, had orchestrated yet another miracle. I was utterly overwhelmed by the situation; indeed, I still find it difficult to put into words how incredible the experience was. Thus, Angus was better able to express the joy, appreciation and excitement we felt about the journey. So, I present you with his touching email to me, and his heartfelt summation of his adventure, which was extremely well received by the Cilfynydd club:

> 27 September 2005
>
> Dad,
>
> It will be a lot of fun and incredibly exciting. I can understand you find it hard to believe it is happening. But start to believe Big Boy; it's not long to go and it is *happening*.
>
> If however you find it hard to understand this, perhaps I can explain the way I see it. As I'm sure you are aware, I am incredibly proud of what you achieved as an All Black (who wouldn't be). But now, looking back at what you and Mum went through, that was a much greater achievement. No one else outside of the family could possibly understand that.
>
> Anyway, I still remember as a 12–13 year old boy going to the flea market with you on a Saturday morning at some ungodly hour, selling the pots you and Mum had made and also the mice that I made. Perhaps more importantly I still remember … (*Stop!* Just to let you know I am at home with the kids for the school holidays. I have just burst into tears and moved away from the computer about three times because I haven't been able to finish this. Even sent Lyn in Christchurch a text and she has burst into tears in a café). *Right.* Got myself together again. As I was saying, I vividly remember the day you decided to take your rugby jerseys to the flea market. I remember saying, 'Dad, you can't do this.' And you explained to me that you and Mum needed the money. I didn't really understand at the time. I can still see the rugby jerseys hanging on the wall of the New World carpark.

Well, as time went by I have explained this story to a few close friends and said that one day I was going to track down that All Black jersey of yours that was in Wales somewhere. Now this is where the *journey* begins (I sound like John Mitchell). There have been three people that have been integral in this trip of ours eventuating, all very close friends of mine.

Two years ago I was having a beer with Jan Maruska when he was down from Auckland for the Sevens and I explained the story to him. He said to me, 'Angus, you have to go and find that jersey of your dad's otherwise you will be sitting here in a few years still telling the same story and it will eat away at you.' Well I couldn't have agreed more. However, another year passed and when Jan came down to the Sevens this year, we got talking again and I realised a whole year had passed and nothing had happened.

The second person integral in this whole affair is Donald Stott. Coincidently, I was having a drink and a chat with him on 1 May 2005 (your birthday) and was telling him that I was going to find that jersey. We talked quite a bit about it and then I suddenly realised it was your birthday. I said to Donald, 'Right, I'm going to do it.'

Donald said to me, 'Angus, stop talking about it and *just do it*.' So we decided that I would ring you on your birthday and your birthday present would be a trip to Wales to get the jersey back if the club over there would allow it. I'm sure you remember the phone call I made that day.

The rest of the story relates to tracking down the jersey (which took a while). Again, wasn't it quite unbelievable that I got an email from Nigel Jones that night when you were staying and I rang him. The rest is history and it just so happens that our trip has coincided with some All Black games. Very fitting indeed.

The remaining person in this whole story is of course Lyn. When I got home that night of 1 May 2005 and explained to her what I had done, she simply said, 'What a fantastic idea.' I'm sure, no, I *know* there would be plenty of wives out there that would have blown their nut for not discussing it with them first. She has been very supportive of the whole thing *all the way*. As you know Lyn is very frugal with money and not once has she asked how much this was going to cost. Later on I asked her if she would like to come too but she turned down the opportunity due to school commitments. Again, I don't know how many people, given the choice, would decide that.

Dad, I have had a lot of correspondence from Nigel Jones of the Cilfynydd club in Wales. He was particularly keen to make sure that we are there for the full day prior to the Welsh test (we will be). He has said he is working hard to make the day a memorable one. A lot of the club members are looking forward to the day and there will be a representative from the Welsh Rugby Union along with current and former players of the Cilfynydd Rugby Club. Perhaps we better give some thought to a speech but given what I have just gone through writing this email, if I was to do it, it might end up in tears again. In any case it would definitely be more appropriate coming from you. Perhaps you might want to give this some thought. I'm not sure what they have got planned but best be prepared.

Well, I think that pretty much sums it up. I am really looking forward to it. It will be fantastic (tears going again). I am just extremely fortunate, and I mean *extremely*, to be in a position to be able to do this. I guess the emotive nature of this email might give you some idea of what this means to me. And to be honest, this is not about me (I mean it). That jersey is a very unique piece of MacEwan family history and may never be repeated by another MacEwan. So Dad let's go have some fun and enjoy the whole expedition.

I will copy Mum in on this email after you have read it first.

Love to you both,

Angus (27 September 2005)

PS. (Tears going again as I push the send button. I can't remember the last time I cried like this; some emotive button has been pushed inside me *big time*).

Angus Sums up the Trip

> The club in Wales put on an absolutely amazing function and arranged for Welsh Rugby Union officials to be there, a Welsh choir, current and past players as well as one of the British Lions that Dad played against in 1959. An absolutely amazing evening and one I will never forget. The club did not go empty-handed as prior to our departure I approached my brother-in-law, Josef Schmidt, who was the Auckland Blues back coach at the time, and requested he approach some of the All Blacks to see if they would be kind enough to donate one of their jerseys so that we could give it to the Cilfynydd Club. All Black Joe Rokocoko provided one of his and this was handed to the club at the function.
>
> One thing I realised as a result of all of this was that the return of the jersey meant more to me than it did to Dad. I think the reason for this is that Dad had achieved the highest level that one could achieve in rugby becoming an All Black and that could never be taken away from him, jersey or no jersey. I was never going to be an All Black and perhaps this is why it meant more to me. This is an incredible story and the trip that Dad and I shared was nothing short of amazing. I shouldn't have any regrets but I do. I only wish that my wonderful mother and my wife had come with us.

Joe Rooney was so inspired by Angus' efforts he dedicated his second poem to him:

A Special Son

> This is the story of a jersey,
> The colour—just 'all black'
> And a long quest by a son
> To get his dad's jersey back.
>
> Worn by his father
> Who realised a boyhood dream
> To play for the 'All Blacks'
> Where they would reign supreme.

The jersey found its way to Wales
To a little mining town
Where it was displayed on the Cilfynydd wall
A true jewel in its crown.

After 38 years the search has ended,
The jersey is back where its journey began.
But it had formed enduring friendships
With this little mining town;
The persistence of son, Angus,
Who answered an inner call,
Now that much-loved jersey
Adorns the MacEwans' studio wall.

The prodigal has returned
To its rightful place,
And a smile has returned
To a special lady's face.

There were many demons,
But that battle has been won;
There is a contented look on an old warrior's face
Thanks to a special son.

When Joe presented the poems to me in his home in Waikanae, to my surprise he also gave me Roddy Evans's 1959 Test jersey that had travelled home via Perth in Australia. The Springbok jersey is still on display in the trophy cabinet in Cilfynydd, Wales.

THE ALL BLACK AND THE LION WENT TO CILFYNYDD: RODDY EVANS REFLECTS ON OUR VISIT TO WALES

What a great weekend it was. First of all finding out through the newspaper that Nev was in Wales, ringing him up and, for the first time in almost 50 years, talking to the man I marked in those 1959 Test matches. He told me about the jersey, and the dinner arranged for the Friday evening at Cilfynydd. Within a short time he had arranged for me and my son Bas to accompany him and his son Angus to the dinner.

On Friday evening we set off from Porthcawl to meet Nev and Angus at the Cilfynydd Rugby Club. I had never been to Cilfynydd before. The night was going to be Nev's special night, but I was also given the warmest of welcomes. I was proud to be a Welshman with the greeting Nev and Angus received. There is a warmth and friendship in the Welsh valleys, and never more than when rugby is involved. The evening was magnificent: splendid food, good speeches and a great Welsh male voice choir. One of the things that struck me was the number of Cilfynydd youth there, and their first-class behaviour throughout the evening.

The highlight of the evening was when Nev came forward to receive his old jersey, and to the surprise of all he presented the club with an All Black jersey from the New Zealand Rugby Union signed by the flying Joe Rokocoko. Our weekend was complete with Nev coming to our church in Porthcawl on Sunday morning, and speaking from the front to all those attending. It was a special few days never to be forgotten. I'm almost ready now to forgive Nev for the hard times he gave me in those test matches!

Sadly, Roddy died after a short battle with health issues and is survived by his wife, Sue, sons Nigel and Bas, and four grandchildren. His funeral was on 24 November 2017 and the WRU passed on the heartfelt condolences of Welsh rugby to the family.

I will never forget the night at Cilfynydd and it emphasised for me the biblical truth that if we give freely it will return in a larger measure than we can ever imagine…

> Give, and it will be given to you. A good measure, pressed down, shaken together and running over, will be poured into your lap. For with the measure you use, it will be measured to you (Luke 6:38 NIV).

7. Spiritual Awakening

> Show me people who drink too much, who have to try out fancy drinks, and I will show you people who are miserable and sorry for themselves, always causing trouble and always complaining. Their eyes are bloodshot, and they have bruises that could have been avoided.
>
> Don't let wine tempt you, even though it is rich red, and it sparkles in the cup, and it goes down smoothly. The next morning you will feel as if you had been bitten by a poisonous snake. Weird sights will appear before your eyes, and you will not be able to think or speak clearly. You will feel as if you were out on the ocean, seasick, swinging high up in the rigging of a tossing ship. 'I must have been hit,' you will say; 'I must have been beaten up, but I don't remember it. Why can't I wake up? I need another drink' (Proverbs 23:29–35 GNT).

Introduction: A New Dawn

> What you believe and focus on becomes your reality.
> Michael McMillan

Prior to my confronting my alcoholism, I blamed everyone I believed had hurt me, or betrayed my confidence. I never took ownership of my decisions, or choices. My problems were always someone else's doing and not my responsibility. My old way of dealing with my problems had to be totally thrown overboard. I began to realise the choices I make today lay the foundation of my future.

- What I sow, I will reap
- What I think, I will become
- What I hate, I will be

As you will see when we delve deeper into this chapter, I decided to start living by trudging the tough, but ultimately happy, road of destiny via the Alcoholics Anonymous (AA) '12-Step Programme'.

THE 12-STEP PROGRAMME

AA's famous, and highly successful step-by-step guide to sobriety (below), was put together in 1935 by a reformed alcoholic ('Bill') and a Pentecostal minister ('Dr Bob').

1) We admitted we were powerless over alcohol—that our lives had become unmanageable
2) Came to believe that a Power greater than ourselves could restore us to sanity
3) Made a decision to turn our will and our lives over to the care of God as we understood Him
4) Made a searching and fearless moral inventory of ourselves
5) Admitted to God, to ourselves, and to another human being the exact nature of our wrongs
6) Were entirely ready to have God remove all these defects of character
7) Humbly asked Him to remove our shortcomings
8) Made a list of all persons we had harmed, and became willing to make amends to them all
9) Made direct amends to such people wherever possible, except when to do so would injure them or others
10) Continued to take personal inventory and when we were wrong promptly admitted it

11) Sought through prayer and meditation to improve our conscious contact with God, as we understood Him, praying only for knowledge of His will for us and the power to carry that out.

12) Having had a spiritual awakening as the result of these steps, we tried to carry this message to alcoholics, and to practice these principles in all our affairs

The AA work generally known as *The Big Book* has numerous insights and words of wisdom which inspired me. Hence, I will be quoting from it and from the Bible throughout this chapter.

> Rarely have we seen a person fail who has thoroughly followed our path. Those who do not recover are people who cannot or will not completely give themselves to this simple program, usually men and women who are constitutionally incapable of being honest with themselves. If you have decided you want what we have and are willing to go to any length to get it—then you are ready to take certain steps.[16]

I wanted change in my life, and I was willing to do anything to accomplish that. You will see that living out the 12 Steps and making myself better was tough. Moreover, getting honest with myself after years of self-neglect, was testing, but ultimately rewarding. Each step along the path to wellness is a deeply personal journey.

Some parts of the programme may be easier to grasp than others for certain people. Nevertheless, one's total recovery from addiction requires absolute commitment to each step every day or you fail to find peace within, or what we call *serenity*. The result of emphasising one step over another, or leaving a step or steps out altogether ends with the addict returning in a bigger way to their addiction.

---

16 Alcoholics Anonymous, (2001). Alcoholics Anonymous: The Big Book (p. 58). New York, NY: AA World Services Inc.

Thus, without further ado, join me in my story of spiritual awakening.

> Turning problems into solutions requires that we adjust our perception, suspend our judgments, and remain open-minded to all possibilities. In other words, it means seeing reality for what it 'really' is and for what it 'really' isn't. Michael McMillan

Part 1: Alcohol, Shame and Suicide Attempt

> Forgetting what is behind ... I press on toward the goal to win the prize. Philippians 3:13–14 NIV

In 1979, I was charged by the New Zealand Police for 'theft as a servant related to accounting practices associated with the Manawatu Branch of the National Travel Association.'

I was ashamed, frightened, helpless and crushed. I couldn't tell anyone or seek help, even from my lawyer. I drank heavily pretending the nightmare would go away, but it didn't. As my day in court approached I couldn't face the situation. So I tried to take my life to end the nightmare I was going through. It's safe to say the life I had created, by my own bad choices, had turned to a living hell.

I had no ill-feelings towards the people who brought the charges against me. They had a responsibility to do what they did. Ironically, their concerns saved me, and brought me face to face with a stark reality. I was an alcoholic like my father. Thus, as a result of my attempted suicide, accident and emergency doctors and my lawyer quickly assessed my problems and promptly placed me in a secure environment. So, my spiritual journey started in Ward 5 (the detox ward for drug and alcohol patients) of the Palmerston North Hospital. It was here I reluctantly went to my first Alcoholics Anonymous[17] meeting with a shocking attitude.

---
17 Alcoholics Anonymous call free number 0800 229 675

I thought I knew all there was to know about AA, after all my dad had been one of the founding members. I'd been paraded around all manner of meetings, and spoken at numerous events with my mother and brothers. I should be the person encouraging 'them' to turn their lives around. The charge nurse who knew my background encouraged me to attend. I went along at her request; I could always tell her later it wasn't for me.

'Hello, my name is Neven, and I am an alcoholic.'

As it turned out the Monday night meeting didn't take place. The guys who usually came in to take the meeting rang in saying they couldn't make it. This gave me the excuse I needed. I told everyone I wasn't interested anyway, if their cancellation was any indication of their commitment to the programme. This outburst of self-righteous indignation displayed how arrogant I had become in avoiding the truth of my desperate situation.

Nevertheless, the nursing staff didn't give up, and encouraged me to attend the following week. I begrudgingly went to the meeting little knowing I would meet my future AA sponsor, Robin. He arrived with two other guys, and we began the meeting with the Serenity Prayer. Then, Robin shared his struggles, and made a statement which has lived with me to this day: 'Alcoholism is a disease. You are at dis-ease with yourself.'

The penny didn't just drop, it sparked something in my heart. The statement was me to a T. I'd been dogged by self-doubt all my life. My public face of All Black, teacher, businessman, civic leader and family man was a mask. Behind it was a broken, frightened and deeply confused person. Hence, from this moment on I was determined to find the real Neven MacEwan. Giving up alcohol became my first priority. Robin would be my guide on the journey to sobriety for over three years.

Inside of us all lurks an ape or an angel. The one we feed survives, so we must be vigilant so that the ape does not block out the light and take over. This is why the AA encourages alcoholics to make a public declaration: once the subject is in the open it no longer controls us. Step 1 of the 12-Step Programme is admitting we were powerless over alcohol—that our lives had become unmanageable.

Another first step on my path to recovery with AA was uttering the famous declaration, 'Hello, my name is Neven, and I am an alcoholic.'

I recited the line many times in the month I remained in Ward 5, and countless more times in the years ahead. During this time my life would be exposed nationwide in the press, radio and television. I lost my reputation, self-respect, business and was informed by my accountant and lawyer that my family's home would have to be sold to pay all of my creditors. In fact, they suggested I considered declaring myself bankrupt. My lawyer told me even on his salary he would not have been able to maintain the repayments on the mortgages, so selling up was the only realistic option.

Part 2: My Spiritual Awakening Begins

I believe all addictive behaviour has three core elements at its root: selfishness, greed and bitterness. To fully recover, three new elements of life must dominate our existence: forgiveness serving others and contentment.

As I started really listening to what others were saying, I began to learn who I really was. As a result I eventually found my true gifts and strengths. In Ward 5, I admitted I was powerless over alcohol. My life had become unmanageable and I knew one drink was never going to be enough. Initially, when I came out of the Ward I was unable to walk past a hotel, or pub without shaking uncontrollably. I was forced to cross the road because being near alcohol started a journey of destructive thoughts.

> For those who are unable to drink moderately the question is how to stop altogether. We are assuming, of course, that the reader desires to stop. Whether such a person can quit upon a non— spiritual basis depends upon the extent to which he has already

> lost the power to choose drink or not. Many of us felt that we had plenty of character. There was a tremendous urge to cease forever. Yet we found it impossible. This is the baffling feature of alcoholism as we know it—this utter inability to leave it alone, no matter how great the necessity or the wish.[18]

That described me and I understood what I needed to do—I could never drink alcohol again.

> So our troubles we think are basically of our own making. They arise out of ourselves, and the alcohol is an extreme example of self-will run riot, though he usually doesn't think so. Above everything else we alcoholics must be rid of this selfishness. We must, or it will kill us. God makes that possible.[19]

I had to make a firm resolution I was never going to drink alcohol again and admit my poor self-control had run riot. If I did drink, my life would again become unmanageable. I would not be able to cope with day-to-day living that required positive decisions to be made. The alcoholic by being numb to reality puts off the hard decisions by procrastinating. I found making decisions—and being responsible for those decisions—was something quite new especially when dealing with facts rather than emotions.

Nevertheless, it took a lot of hard work and effort to change my thinking. You already know of my sponsor Robin and his help, but the fellowship, prayers and Bible readings of the Christian support group I eventually joined, and which I shall discuss in-depth later on, was of immense help.

> Our description of the alcoholic… Make clear three pertinent ideas: that we were alcoholic and could not manage our own lives; that probably no human power could have relieved our alcoholism; and that God could and would if he were sought.[20]

---

18 *Big Book*, p. 34
19 *Big Book*, p. 62
20 *Big Book*, p. 60

A vital part of the AA programme is undergoing a spiritual awakening for only then would peace and security be found. The programme is a process and there are no instant answers or solutions. The alcoholic doesn't stop being a drunk because he is no longer drinking, sobriety is a journey not a destination.

Thus, Step 2 played an important role in giving me a powerful form of support when I 'came to believe that a Power greater than myself could restore me to sanity.' The founders of Alcoholics Anonymous realised that only by accepting a power higher than ourselves is recovery possible.

> Remember we deal with alcohol—cunning, baffling, powerful! Without help it is too much for us. But there is One who has all power—that One is God. May you find Him now![21]

I had to learn not to play God in my life. My direction had led to disaster so it was for the best I gave myself over to a higher power. AA's *Big Book* reminded me of this fact:

> First of all we had to quit playing God. It didn't work. Next, we decided that hereafter in this drama of life, God was going to be our Director. He is the Principal; we are His agents. He is the Father, and we are His children. Most good ideas are simple, and this concept was the keystone of the new triumphant arch through which we passed to freedom.[22]

Reinforcing this spiritual aspect the AA meetings open and close with the Serenity Prayer:

> God grant me the serenity to accept the things I cannot change, courage to change the things I can, and wisdom to know the difference.

---

21 *Big Book*, p. 58
22 *Big Book*, p. 62

It took me a while to fully appreciate the full meaning of the prayer, and I'll discuss its importance to me in Part III. Nevertheless, one thing I had begun to appreciate was the notion of God acting through the kindness and support of others.

Your Mentors are God's Guides

Every member of the AA chooses a sponsor or mentor, someone who has themselves been an alcoholic because they have an empathy and understanding of the process of recovering from a lifetime's addiction. This person benefits from the relationship as it affirms their own journey and inspires patience and perseverance.

> Practical experience shows that nothing will so much ensure immunity from drinking as intensive work with alcoholics. It works when other activities fail … You can help when no one else can. You can secure their confidence when others fail. Remember they are very ill.[23]

Robin remained my sponsor and mentor for three years and I learnt a tremendous amount from him. He would appear at the door as if from nowhere when I was going through a down time, and gave of his time helping me out of my dilemma. They were God-given moments because, he had not been prompted to call in and see me. As you will see, God truly works in mysterious and marvellous ways.

Part 3: My Quest to Find 'I Am'

Step 3 of the AA programme which involved 'accepting the God of my understanding,' was a fairly easy process. I had first been involved in the church while a boarder at Wellesley College where I was a chorister. During Dad's turbulent, troubled times my brothers and I were encouraged by Mum to attend Sunday School so she could have time out. I was sometimes highly enthusiastic about church, and at other times quite ambivalent.

---

23 *Big Book*, p. 89

Later, while attending Nelson College, morning assembly always started with a hymn, Bible reading and prayer. During my last year at Nelson College when I became a boarder we had to attend church every Sunday. Yet church didn't hold any great meaning to me, it was just one of those things you did. So, apart from my marriage in 1958 at St Matthew's in Dunedin, and my children's baptisms, church life, even God, held no significance for me.

Now, while the second step had asked me to believe only that a power greater than myself could restore me to sanity, I embraced the God of my understanding easily at this point. It wasn't long before I was confronted with the real God, the 'I AM', Jesus. Now, I shall detail how He found me.

THE LINE IS DRAWN

When I eventually left Ward 5, I had decided the best plan for us as a family would be to flee to South Africa and start a new life. It didn't figure in my thinking I had no money because, I had always managed to find it in the past when I needed it. Jeannette finally put her foot down declaring:

> No more! It's time you faced the music. Running away is not going to change you; all you'll be doing is taking the problem to a different place.

With this one comment, I began to truly understand AA's Serenity Prayer I'd been reciting since Ward 5...

When talking to my heavenly Father I asked him what it is I cannot change, and what are the things I can. A while later, I found reading the full Serenity Prayer as written by Reinhold Niebuhr (1892-1971); it gave greater insight. The latter part, in particular, would eventually help me understand myself. The rest of the Serenity Prayer reads...

> Living one day at a time; enjoying one moment at a time; accepting hardships as the pathway to peace; taking, as He did, this sinful world as it is, not as I would have it; trusting that He will make all things right if I surrender to His Will; that I may be reasonably

happy in this life and supremely happy with Him forever in the next. Amen.[24]

I then discovered the 10 unchangeable factors in my life. My:

- Physical features
- Natural parents
- Brothers and sisters
- Race and nationality
- Mental capacity
- Time in history
- Gender
- Birth order
- Aging process
- Death

I needed to avoid cosmetic changes and uproot deep-rooted problems. Otherwise, I would never fulfil my true potential. As a child I would tell myself I was no good, a failure, and feel inferior. I became envious of others, and found it difficult to return genuine affection. These feelings led me down the path of self-condemnation. I would inevitably gravitate downwards to where I would be accepted—the pit of destruction.

What the above 10 factors boil down to is my *thinking*. If, I change the way I *think* it changes my attitude. When my attitude changes, my behaviour changes. This can only happen with humility and by God's good grace. He's so willing to help, but I had to change my thinking about Him and allow Him to take over my life. This meant living by the 49 commands[25] of Jesus Christ, which changed my character and my way of doing things.

---

24 Retrieved from https://www.beliefnet.com/prayers/protestant/addiction/serenity-prayer.aspx
25 Authored by the Institute in Basic Life Principles. See https://iblp.org/news/commands-christ-series

For Richer or Poorer

Everyone had been telling Nettie to leave me, including the business community in Palmerston North, her family and even my brothers: 'He is no good—a loser and will only drag you down into his quagmire.'

But Jeannette didn't leave me, and without her I wouldn't have made it. Reflecting on those tumultuous days, I am full of admiration and humbled by her commitment to me and the family. It was a little later in 1981 when I plucked up the courage to ask her why she hadn't left me. Jeannette was in no doubt:

> When we were married at St Matthew's church, I promised before God, 'For better or worse, for richer or poorer, in sickness and in health, till death us do part.' Well, things couldn't get any worse or poorer, so there was no choice.

I Was in Hospital and You Visited Me

> *Without change, there is no innovation, creativity, or incentive for improvement. Those who initiate change will have a better opportunity to manage the change that is inevitable.*
> William G. Pollard

In hospital, I had visits from church leaders from three different denominations: John and Yvonne Walton who were pastors of the New Life Church, Monsignor Tom Duffy from the Catholic church, and the Reverend David Penman, vicar of All Saints Parish. I first met John Walton when organising 'Carols by Candlelight' for the Public Relations Office in 1977. I was approached by a group of Christian leaders to help organise and find sponsorship for the event. Convinced of my authority and leadership, I agreed to their funding proposals. Nevertheless, I warned that in the event of bad weather I alone decided whether the event went ahead or not.

On Sunday morning (the day of the event), the weather was shocking. I believed the event had to be postponed or cancelled, and

2.00 pm was my deadline to say yes or no. The organising group called at my office and asked me to pray with them for the weather to clear. I thought they were crazy and said, 'You've got to be joking.' Then they prayed in a way I'd never experienced before. The weather cleared and the event went ahead. A miracle had happened. Someone, it seemed, had far more authority than I did. I didn't let on, but I was deeply troubled by the experience.

Anyhow, John's wife Yvonne visited me, and she gave me a book called *Born Again* written by Chuck Colson, President Nixon's legal advisor who served time in prison for his part in the Watergate scandal. The book had a profound impact on me and I knew as I read it in some way I was going to be working with those in prison. Ironically, it was the last place I wanted to be, especially as an inmate. Furthermore, I had no idea the Lord would have plans for Mr Colson and I.

The vicar of All Saints, David Penman visited me and, after chatting for some time, asked if he could pray for me. He then left returning the next day. I noticed all these Christians had something which was quite amazing. They genuinely cared and had such a serenity about them. I was humbled by their non-judgmental support and I desired what they had, whatever the cost.

Monsignor Tom Duffy brought something quite unique to the situation: good old-fashioned humour. I had known of Tom in Wellington in my rugby days but never in relation to the spiritual needs of life. He came into Ward 5 large as life and profoundly stated I wouldn't go to prison even though a seven-year sentence was possible. If I did, he promised, to walk down Broadway carrying a 'Sally Army' (Salvation Army) banner in front of their band on a Sunday night. Tom got me laughing at myself again and accepting whatever the outcome of my foolish choices might be.

I was intensely emotional about what God was doing through AA. So I invited a few Christians to our home to share what God was doing in my life. In my naivety, I told them the AA philosophy was the future church: 'Come to the God of your understanding, and he will fix all your problems. It is a church which gives immediate solutions to all manner of ailments.' One of my visitors replied in a very loving and quiet manner, 'But you can't just go to God. There is a way.' Nothing else was said, but the comment puzzled me.

I AM Who I AM
I had accepted the God of my understanding and I might have been ready to accept Jesus as a great moral teacher. Nevertheless, to accept His claim to be the way, the truth and the life! Well, it was going to be a real challenge. The next morning in my prayer and devotional time I opened my Bible and there was the verse of scripture which told me the way:

> Jesus answered him, 'I am the way, the truth, and the life;
> no one goes to the Father except by me (John 14:6).

C S Lewis, that great writer of books like *The Screwtape Letters*, had the answer for me in this quote from *Mere Christianity*:[26]

> I am trying here to prevent anyone saying the really foolish thing that people often say about Him: I'm ready to accept Jesus as a great moral teacher, but I don't accept his claim to be God. That is the one thing we must not say. A man who was merely a man and said the sort of things Jesus said would not be a great moral teacher. He would either be a lunatic—on the level with the man who says he is a poached egg—or else he would be the Devil of Hell. You must make your choice. Either this man was, and is, the Son of God, or else a madman or something worse. You can shut him up for a fool, you can spit at him and kill him as a demon or you can fall at his feet and call him Lord and God, but let us not come with any patronizing nonsense about his being a great human teacher. He has not left that open to us. He did not intend to.

I had finally found the great I AM. Hence, I made my choice and accepted Jesus as my Saviour, my Lord, my God, my Higher Power.

---

26 Retrieved from https://www.goodreads.com/work/quotes/801500-mere-christianity

I likened this wonderful historical event to God calling Moses to lead His people out of Egypt.

> But Moses replied, 'When I go to the Israelites and say to them, "The God of your ancestors sent me to you," they will ask me, "what is his name?" So what can I tell them?' God said, 'I am who I am. You must tell them: "The one who is called I AM has sent me to you"' (Exodus 3:13–14 GNT).

At my next AA meeting I had an opportunity to share and I stated, 'I'm nothing, a nobody.' This comment alarmed the group and the members, and in their haste to assure me my statement was incorrect, cut me off mid-sentence: 'Nev, you're an ex-All Black. Yes, you are an alcoholic, but you can become someone again. We're here for you mate.' When they had finished trying to console me I smiled politely, and completed what I had been trying to say: 'On my own, I'm nothing, but in Jesus I'm everything.'

Part IV: Court Appearance and Sentencing

My day in court brought everything into perspective. On 11 July 1979, my wife, my three boys, mother and Vicar David Penman were there to support me. My lawyer, David McKegg, represented me with arguments and explanations for my behaviour. The process was straightforward as I openly admitted to the offending practices. Nettie had no idea what was going on. She did not know our financial situation, nor the quantities of alcohol I was drinking. She had suspected I was a heavy drinker, but it wasn't a problem.

It can be quite easy for an alcoholic to hide the extent of their drinking if they have a busy social life; shallow friendships prevent accountability or awkward questions being asked. So in terms of making the decision that I was powerless over alcohol, it helped that I was in hospital where no alcohol was allowed. Certainly, for me, it was a safe environment. I stayed there during my court case so there was plenty of ongoing support.

In a sense it was very selfish of me to stay in hospital because Nettie then had to carry all the pressure of bringing up the family. It was all on her shoulders. She had to deal with the sale of the business and the lawyers. All I had to do was sign the documents which came in. Not only had I lost my self-respect, I'd lost my business as well.

I was saddened as I began to realise just what I had done to my family. Alcoholism had been like a prison, removing me from the normal range of emotional responses and responsibilities.

> The family of an alcoholic longs for a return to happiness and security. They remember when father was romantic, thoughtful and successful. Today's life is measured against that of other years and, when it falls short, the family may be unhappy... But the head of the house has spent years in pulling down the structures of business, romance, friendship, health—these things are now ruined or damaged. It will take time to clear away the wreck. Though old buildings will eventually be replaced by finer ones, the new structures will take years to complete.[27]

I was always trying to be what I thought others wanted me to be. When I played rugby I was told to be a man, be more physical, and yet it wasn't me. My real character was gentleness and it wasn't to be realised until the process of recovery was well established. Finally, I was coming to terms with my life, and it was vital I had people who understood my battle and could help me.

I was given a reprieve by the court; they did not impose a custodial sentence, but a $500 fine—which just added to my already substantial debts. I knew there was nowhere to go except up. My plummet into hell had finally ended. However, my ascent required years of soul-searching and forgiveness from many people.

---

27 *Big Book*, p. 123

David Penman, the vicar of All Saints, helped me find a job as a farmhand at Keebles Farm, Massey University. I started to go along to AA and church meetings as often as I could; indeed, I recall attending 11 spiritually themed meetings a week. Some may think that was too many. Yet, when drinking, I had regularly attended a variety of spiritual houses (of a different nature) more than eleven times a week. That worship had been expensive and ultimately depressing. These new spiritual exercises were beneficial and free. The deep inner joy and peace I experienced was totally different from everything else I had tried to fill the emptiness within me.

New Habits

However, changing the habits of a lifetime is not easy. Attending church regularly for the first time since my schooldays was foreign and scary. I'll give you an example of how irrational and self-centred my thinking was. It sounds silly now, but I honestly thought the church would fall down on my head.

I learnt that God is personally interested in me, as He is with all his creations. I am nothing special, but He had a purpose and a plan for my life, providing I was prepared to slowly and effectively follow the life pattern of obedience. So I began to learn that faith is not religious practices and works, but developing a relationship of trust in and obedience to Jesus and this is a process. I cried out for help; He heard my cry and amazing things happened.

I began to take it one day, one step, at a time and every day walk purposefully towards sobriety and inner peace, a journey which would take the rest of my life. However, it would not be a lonely one. I began looking for opportunities to serve others which were unimaginable to me in those dark days of despair in 1979.

My debts on the family home were huge, and there seemed no alternative but to sell the property. I did not want to kick my family out of their home, but the debt repayments were financially crippling. I went into the attic of our home and cried out to God:

> Please don't kick my family out of their home. I never wanted to do this; forgive my stupidity. If there is a way to keep our home, show me!

It took seven years of hard work and sacrifice to repay all the debt, yet we stayed in the family home until we sold it in 1994. While there was no easy answer to my financial problems—no benevolent benefactor was going to give me a bag of money or offer me another Golden Product opportunity. Staying in our house posed financial difficulties only God could solve. Yet thanks to Nettie and God, new skills and talents I had never used emerged.

Part V: There's None So Blind as Those Who Will Not See

Before I go on, let me indulge in some Kiwi culture from the 70s which has been overlooked in contemporary society.

Pottery became a very big thing back in the 70s in New Zealand. Indeed, New Zealand's first real smash hit in art and craft came via our potters. In 1976, Nettie had started learning how to make pottery through the adult pottery classes at Freyberg High School. She found she had a natural gift and eventually her creative abilities were acknowledged in 1983 when a pot she entered into the Fletcher Brownbuilt Exhibition was accepted into the competition.

This event ran from 1972 to 1998 and, alongside Mino in Japan and Faenza in Italy, it was one of the biggest three competitions on the world pottery stage. Indeed, works from the golden age of Kiwi pottery now sell for thousands of dollars across the world. Thus, Nettie was a big deal, and still makes outstanding pieces today. Nevertheless, she wasn't involved in pottery to be a name. Nettie does it because she is passionate about it. Her commitment to her craft and me were pivotal in my new life.

A year before my downfall Nettie had progressed to the stage of having a potter's wheel, kiln and work studio in the back section of our double garage at 475 Church Street. So she was making pots, bowls, casserole dishes, storage jars, and coffee mugs by the hundreds.

Sometime after my trial she asked, 'Would you like to try making some moulded bowls for pot plants, and fruit bowls for the table?'

I politely declined as playing with clay wasn't my thing, but she wouldn't take no for an answer. So I decided to give it a go. I was very reluctant, mind you, and I did it so I could say later, 'Nettie, this isn't really my thing.' Remember, in Part I of this chapter, the nurses in Ward 5 had encouraged me to take part in the AA meetings in much the same way, and I'd been just as doubtful.

So Nettie showed me how to make a moulded bowl which could be used as a fruit bowl for a table or dresser. Balls of clay were rolled into the size of an old 10-cent piece, or a dollar in today's coinage. These balls were flattened in the bowl mould and closely packed together. A thin lining of the bowl was then shaped and smoothed over, and finally the rim trimmings were added; these were worms of clay woven together to give a decorative fringe to the finished bowl.

The day ended with my first bowl completed; it needed to dry in its mould for 48 hours. When that time was up I gently took the bowl out of the mould. Now it was set aside to dry thoroughly. After the bisque firing, the inside was glazed and the outside was given an iron oxide wash. The result was an earthen green, glossy, glazed inner, with the brown pattern showing up on the outside. I thought the finished bowl which emerged from the kiln looked surprisingly impressive, but I'd still tell Nettie potting wasn't my thing. I had more pressing matters at hand.

Then something rather incredible happened. An old friend suddenly called in. Micki Shuttleworth was her maiden name. In fact, Micki had been my first girlfriend at Nelson College and she had lived in Wakefield at that time. Nettie and Micki were very good friends. Micki told Nettie the fruit bowl was lovely and asked if she could buy it? Clearly, she thought Nettie had made it. Nettie replied, 'You will have to ask the potter who made it.' Neven! Micki's response was one of surprise, but she came and asked me if I would sell it to her. Well, I had no idea of the value so I slipped out and asked Jeannette what was a realistic price to ask for the bowl and she suggested $20. Micki readily agreed and purchased the bowl.

You would have thought by now I would have seen God getting in on the venture. Smiling, I shook my head and said, 'There's none so blind as those who will not see.'

The next day Micki was back placing an order for three more bowls. So I decided that 'playing around with clay' was certainly for me. In a few days, I had earned $80 towards the budget needed to keep our house. In the next fortnight some 60 orders for bowls flooded in, and I became committed to the creation of pots every spare minute I had. As a result, whenever Nettie shared her experiences with Jesus via the Bible, she always related the potter in the book of Jeremiah back to me.

> The LORD said to me, 'Go down to the potter's house, where I will give you my message.' So I went there and saw the potter working at his wheel. Whenever a piece of pottery turned out imperfect, he would take the clay and make it into something else. Then the LORD said to me, 'Don't I have the right to do with you people of Israel what the potter did with the clay? You are in my hands just like clay in the potter's hands ...' (Jeremiah 18:1–6 GNT).

One day I came across this fantastic, moving Christian poem by Beulah V Cornwall.

THE CHOSEN VESSEL
    The Master was searching for a vessel to use;
    On the shelf there were many—which one would He choose?
    'Take me', cried the gold one, 'I'm shiny and bright,
    I'm of great value and I do things just right.
    My beauty and luster will outshine the rest
    And for someone like You, Master, gold would be the best!'

    The Master passed on with no word at all;
    He looked at a silver urn, narrow and tall;

'I'll serve You, dear Master, I'll pour out Your wine,
and I'll be at Your table whenever You dine,
My lines are so graceful, my carvings so true,
And my silver will always compliment You.'

Unheeding the Master passed on to the brass,
It was widemouthed and shallow, and polished like glass.
'Here! Here!' cried the vessel, 'I know I will do,
Place me on Your table for all men to view.'

'Look at me', called the goblet of crystal so clear,
'My transparency shows my contents so dear,
Though fragile am I, I will serve You with pride,
And I'm sure I'll be happy in Your house to abide.'

The Master came next to a vessel of wood,
Polished and carved, it solidly stood.
'You may use me, dear Master', the wooden bowl said,
'But I'd rather You used me for fruit, not for Bread!'

Then the Master looked down and saw a vessel of clay.
Empty and broken it helplessly lay.
No hope had the vessel that the Master might choose,
To cleanse and make whole, to fill and to use.

'Ah! This is the vessel I've been hoping to find,
I will mend and use it and make it all Mine.
I need not the vessel with pride of its self;
Nor the one who is narrow to sit on the shelf;
Nor the one who is bigmouthed and shallow and loud;
Nor one who displays his contents so proud;
Not the one who thinks he can do all things just right;
But this plain earthy vessel filled with My power and might.'

Then gently He lifted the vessel of clay.
Mended and cleansed it and filled it that day.
Spoke to it kindly. There's work you must do,
Just pour out to others as I pour into you.[28]

---

28 Retrieved from http://www.godswork.org/enpoem42.htm

Neven MacEwan

Getting Out of Debt Starts When You Stop Robbing God!

Pride will cost you everything, but leave you with nothing.
Anonymous

I found myself with a job—creating bowls to fill orders—and my faith was growing; I thought I was making progress. Nevertheless, there were deep issues within me God wanted me to hand over to him.

One Friday evening at an AL-Anon meeting a member asked me to join her on a Saturday morning at the city's flea market and sell my wife's pottery seconds. She told me the flea market had helped her financially through difficult times. Once again all my defences went up, and I was about to turn down the offer. You see, when I was a city councillor I had opposed establishing the flea market in the city because I felt it would lower the city's image. Now I was being asked to be part of the markets to sell my wife's pottery seconds. My pride raised its ugly head again: *"What would people think about me?"* Yet, I wound up thinking, *"Who really cares anyway?"* I was after all a convicted criminal by my own admission.

The following Saturday outside Melody's Supermarket on Broadway Avenue, I was with the AL-Anon group setting up my stall at 5.30 am in readiness for customers to buy some lovely pots. I would hardly have called them 'seconds', but Jeannette was not happy with them, and so they were displayed and priced to sell. The flea market closed at midday, and I was amazed at how well the pots sold. As time went by another close, old 'friend' from Nelson emerged: my artistic and creative streak returned. When I began making animal figures, cats, turtles and mice, a not-so-little 'little boy' called Nev from Nelson began smiling again.

There was never a dull moment at the flea market. I took my bowl moulds and worked on making new ones while waiting to make a sale from the stall. My daughter Jeannie was a star, a true blessing. Jeannie, and on occasion her brother Angus when he didn't have sport or other commitments, would get up at 4.30 am on Saturdays and help me out. As you have read in an earlier chapter, my youngest son Angus, as an adult, remembered my having to sell rugby jerseys at this very flea market.

I was there whatever the weather: rain, hail, shine, frost or the famed Palmerston North wind. The latter was always a challenge. I lost count of the stalls I saw getting swept away. Later on, Nettie made 'Meditation Pots', and gave them to me to give away at the market. These pots were made as she meditated on all the Lord was doing in her life. These were beautiful objects, and very special. I would put one of them on display every week and wait for God to bring to the stall the person He wanted me to give the pot to. It was amazing. I never sold anything until the Meditation Bowl had been given away and the sales always matched our needs for the week.

I always knew who God wanted me to give the pots to. They would come to the stall and lovingly pick one up then and very gently put it back down and then walk away, without asking the price. I would wrap the pot and go after them, and give it to them saying, 'Blessings from God.' The expressions on their faces were ones of sheer joy and delight.

The Lord was gracious in changing my attitudes but was also teaching me wonderful principles for living from His Word. These three passages below meant a lot to me at the time and still do.

> Bring the best of the firstfruits of your soil to the house of the LORD your God (Exodus 23:19).

> 'I the LORD do not change. So you, O descendants of Jacob, are not destroyed. Ever since the time of your forefathers you have turned away from my decrees and have not kept them. Return to me, and I will return to you,' says the LORD Almighty. 'But you ask, "How are we to return?"
>
> 'Will a man rob God? Yet you rob me. But you ask, "How do we rob you?"

'In tithes and offerings. You are under a curse—the whole nation of you—because you are robbing me. Bring the whole tithe into the storehouse, that there may be food in my house. Test me in this,' says the LORD Almighty, 'and see if I will not throw open the floodgates of heaven and pour out so much blessing you will not have room enough for it. I will prevent pests from devouring your crops, and the vines in your fields will not cast their fruit,' says the LORD Almighty. 'Then all the nations will call you blessed, for yours will be a delightful land,' says the LORD Almighty (Malachi 3:6–12).

They came to him and said, 'Teacher, we know that you tell the truth, without worrying about what people think. You pay no attention to anyone's status, but teach the truth about God's will for people. Tell us, is it against our Law to pay taxes to the Roman Emperor? Should we pay them or not?'

But Jesus saw through their trick and answered, 'Why are you trying to trap me? Bring a silver coin, and let me see it.' They brought him one, and he asked, 'Whose face and name are these?'

'The Emperor's,' they answered.

So Jesus said, 'Well, then, pay to the Emperor what belongs to the Emperor, and pay to God what belongs to God.'

And they were amazed at Jesus (Mark 12:14–17 GNT).

Part VI: Under New Management

It is in helping others that we find ourselves and experience real joy and fulfilment in our lives. The 12th Step in the AA Programme is:

> Having had a spiritual awakening as the result of these steps, we tried to carry this message of hope to other suffering alcoholics, and practice all these principles in all our affairs.[29]

My farm work at Massey University and as a laboratory technician in the large animal hospital was made available through Neil Bruère.

---

29 *Big Book.*

He was the professor in charge of the Veterinary Science Faculty and farms at the time and I am very grateful for his support. It was my first stint of work at the aforementioned Keebles Farm that played a vitally important therapeutic role in my recovery.

I really did it all: fencing, new gates, repairs to the woolshed, dagging sheep, bridge repairs and construction, cattle stops, tree planting, and grubbing thistles in paddocks. So, riding a pushbike home after a long, hard, physical day's work was tough, but it certainly helped get me fit again. I also realised how important it is to get your body moving in times of depression.

Whilst the pottery reunited me with my youthful creative side, it was my experiences out in the countryside which helped me embrace Nev the child. As a kid, I'd loved the rural life, and my pushbike had been a great means of freedom. I used to rove all over the Nelson area. While doing so, I often pondered my problems and found solutions.

One day, while riding home from Keebles Farm, I found myself entering the same mode of thought I had used when young. Young Nev had reached out and shown me the way to overcome what I call *stinking thinking*. Stinking thinking is the term I apply to self-indulgent, destructive thoughts. We all feel sorry for ourselves at one time or another. However, if we channel these emotions positively, we grow stronger and can turn a bad situation into opportunities. I recalled Mum's comments that, when I was a kid, I'd had the ability to make the best of a bad situation. Somehow I had lost it as an adult.

On the surface, I'd matured. I'd become a teacher, All Black, businessman and city councillor. Yet, internally, I'd overindulged in self-pity and bitterness. Much of this stemmed from my experiences as a child. I celebrated the bitterness and fed the ape. Due to my focusing on being a victim as a child, I deferred responsibility for my actions as an adult. Consequently I forgot about the strengths the boy possessed. He was a sensitive, good-humoured lad who survived. Re-engaging with my younger self and remembering how I had coped proved revelatory.

Some truly amazing miracles happened in the years from 1983 after I was baptised. They occurred after prayer, reading God's scriptures and helping others in need. Jesus had some profound wisdom on this matter:

> Do not judge others, and God will not judge you; do not condemn others, and God will not condemn you; forgive others, and God will forgive you. Give to others, and God will give to you. Indeed, you will receive a full measure, a generous helping, poured into your hands—all you can hold. The measure you use for others is the one that God will use for you (Luke 6:37–38 GNT).

When I spoke about my experiences with Jesus some people were convinced the positive events were coincidences. I always replied these coincidences would stop when I stopped praying, and refused to do what Jesus wanted and desired for me. So I often told people I loved the Lord Jesus and I was under new management. Jesus was now the boss, and I was His agent. Nevertheless, there is a yardstick to check our love for Jesus and that is keeping his commands and reading his word.

> I prayed to the LORD my God and confessed the sins of my people. I said, 'Lord God, you are great, and we honour you. You are faithful to your covenant and show constant love to those who love you and do what you command' (Daniel 9:4 GNT).

> If you obey my commands, you will remain in my love, just as I have obeyed my Father's commands and remain in his love. I have told you this so that my joy may be in you and that your joy may be complete (John 15:10–11 GNT).

The commands Jesus spoke of in John's Gospel are not the Ten Commandments. They are the 49 commands Jesus taught His disciples. These teachings are recorded in the gospels of Matthew, Mark, Luke and John. If you obey these 49 commands your character qualities will be enhanced and you will become a different person entirely.

I was also challenged by Derek Prince, a great Bible teacher, who said, 'We only love Jesus as much as the time we spend reading his word.'

I've been reading ever since.

Discovery and Baptism

> 'I am telling you the truth,' replied Jesus, 'that no one can enter the Kingdom of God without being born of water and the Spirit' (John 3:5 GNT).

Finding out where the Lord wanted me to worship was another great adventure. I went to the Christian Life church which met in the hall at Queen Elizabeth College in Palmerston North. There I met another All Black, John Loveday, who was my chiropractor. John had established his Christianity a long time before me. He was also twenty years younger. Nevertheless, we shared many of the same views and many other things besides. We celebrated our birthdays on the same day. Like me, he had been a lock forward. We would pair up to share our testimonies around the North Island at Full Gospel Businessmen's Fellowship meetings.

I eventually made All Saints my home. Indeed, thanks to David Penman and my family, it had been inviting me in all along. My wife, daughter and youngest son were part of the choir. I was a member of two of the church's house groups which were another important step in my Christian development. The house groups met once every week for Bible study, prayer and fellowship. The first was led by Kevin O'Sullivan and the second by Bob and Margot Greenway. At Kevin O'Sullivan's group, there was a new Christian by the name of Doug Stewart. He was a confident individual who asked questions to which I wanted answers too, and Kevin wisely and patiently explained them all as we searched for the truth. This group gave me a solid foundation for faith to grow. Kevin, a lawyer, was an outstanding teacher and lecturer on scripture.

The other group I joined was Bob and Margot Greenway's, and another step in discovering what it meant to follow Jesus was taken.

It was while attending this group the question about baptism came up. I had been baptised, although obviously, as an infant I didn't have any comprehension of what baptism was about. Now, the possibility of my baptism by full immersion, as a self-aware adult came up. I was encouraged by Bob and Margot to approach David Penman and ask him if he could take my request to the Bishop as I had to wait for approval to be given.

David called me in after the Easter of 1983 and said the Bishop had finally approved my baptism by full immersion. The Bishop had said to David I was, 'affirming my baptism as a child by full immersion.' Nevertheless, it felt like it was my first authentic baptism.

On Saturday night 21 May 1983, I was baptised in a hot tub at the Steffensen's home. It was also mine and Jeannette's wedding anniversary, and the eve of Pentecost Sunday. This is the day the Holy Spirit visited the apostles and those who followed Christ. My new life had begun, the journey of sobriety and discipleship equipped me for what lay ahead; it also enabled me to understand and accept my past.

Manawahe: The Place of New Beginnings

In 1984, I was invited by the Anglican church in Kawerau to take part in a mission outreach. This was organised by Bernie Blakeley, a man small in stature, but a giant in the faith. He was associated with the Kimberley family in Palmerston North through the marriage of his daughter Felicity to Bill Kimberley. Bill Kimberley was a member of the Greenway house group and highly supportive of my faith in its infancy.

The last meeting of the mission was held in a little hall in Manawahe. A very small group was in attendance that night and, at the end of the meeting, Bernie said he sensed the Lord saying, concerning me, 'Lay hands on this man and send him forth in faith with my blessing for the ministry I have for him.'

I left Manawahe, went back to Massey University and gave my notice of resignation. I then readied myself for what the Lord had in store for me in the days ahead. Within six months I was working with Prison Fellowship New Zealand as chairman of the Manawatu Committee. I was then appointed to the role of Executive Director for New Zealand, a position I held up until 1989 when the Lord called me away from this organisation. I was then encouraged to apply for the position of chaplain at Manawatu Prison.

I laughed at this suggestion at first because I knew New Zealand's Justice Department wouldn't appoint anyone with a criminal record. Reluctantly I applied, not really expecting to get an interview. When we think there is no hope, look to the Lord; He does the impossible. I got an interview, was appointed chaplain, and started on 29 October 1989. I held the position until my retirement on 29 October 2005.

The journey to this appointment started in this tiny meeting at Manawahe when the people spoke prophecy from God on me, and then walking in faith with the Lord prepared me to go where he wanted me to go. I strongly believe we don't meet people by accident. When we get our lives together in harmony with the Creator's spirit, He draws people to us by His presence within us. Do you remember when I was recovering in hospital people came to visit me displaying something I didn't have but which I wanted, whatever the cost. When you are desperate you will find the answer within you, and with the people who visit you at the time of need. The crisis in my life was the door of opportunity.

CHUCK COLSON, MICHAEL FOWLER AND ME
Another amazing miracle of the Lord happened in 1986, when I was working with Prison Fellowship of New Zealand as its Executive Director. The founder of Prison Fellowship, Chuck Colson, was visiting New Zealand. Chuck's Watergate story had enthralled me in my early days of sobriety and I was thrilled to finally meet him. Colson arrived in Auckland, undertook engagements with the Auckland committee, then flew to Palmerston North to speak at a mayoral prayer breakfast and to senior pupils at one of the local high schools. He would finally dot down in Wellington for a board meeting capped off by a speaking engagement open to the general public.

Initially, it was planned to hold the Wellington meeting in a church hall, but the committee organising the event asked the Lord if the church hall was where He wanted the meeting held. The answer came back through the collective contributions from the prayer group as a big no. One of the prayer group believed God wanted it held in the Michael Fowler Centre. Instead of a hall that held 100 people God wanted to hold the meeting in a venue that held 5,000. God had spoken.

Everyone thought we were mad, bordering on insane. One sceptic told me we wouldn't get the venue anyway as it is booked years in advance. I contacted the booking office to find out the costings and availability. The only night free for the rest of the year was the night we wanted to hold the public meeting. The cost was $5,000, a lot of money back in 1986. When adjusted for inflation the amount would be something like $13,000 today. We didn't have the money in the bank, or any guarantee the money would be available to pay the deposit of $500, which was required in a week, or the balance which was to be paid seven days after the event.

I booked the venue anyway. I believed God had spoken and the finance required would be supplied in His way and in His timing. The Wellington committee was responsible for promoting the night by notifying churches in the Wellington region and advertising in the papers by having the ads sponsored, or funds raised to cover the costs. The next day an anonymous donation of $500 was received in the mail so the deposit was paid for. Now all we needed was the $5,250 to cover the balance and all other charges. I approached our bank at the time for sponsorship of $5,000 and that proposal was very gracefully declined.

On the day of the meeting, Colson pulled me aside and said how concerned he was about the size and cost of the venue, and the lack of advertising to promote the event. He went on to say if the Michael Fowler Centre was filled it would be equivalent to the miracle of parting the Red Sea when Moses led God's people out of bondage, out of Egypt and into the Promised Land.

He wasn't being melodramatic. Jack Marshall, a former Prime Minister and member of Prison Fellowship's board of trustees, had hosted a function in the Fowler Centre for the former Prime Minister of Great Britain, Edward Heath, the year before. He had had an advertising budget 10 times what we had spent and he charged $50 a seat. However, he attracted only a few hundred people and the auditorium looked empty. We had decided not to make any charge for the night, but would take up an offering to meet our costs. So having no idea how many people would turn up all we could do was to wait and watch what God would do with our offering of loaves and fishes, our step of faith for Him.

The meeting was due to start at 7.30 pm and Nettie and I went down to the Fowler Centre to check the final preparations and meet for prayer to ask God to bless the evening and bring His people to the venue. At 7.00 pm you could have fired a cannon into the Fowler Centre and you wouldn't have hit one person. Nothing had changed by 7.15 pm. But then people started arriving from every direction and all the entrances to the auditorium were packed with people. It was truly amazing where all the people came from and the Fowler Centre was nearly full when the evening started. It was just an amazing night and it took my faith to another level.

But more was yet to come. Before Chuck Colson was asked to address the meeting an offering was collected. Milkshake containers were passed along the rows. These were then gathered up, put into rubbish bags and given to the security guards. The money was then taken away to be handed in the morning to our bank which would count the offering and deposit the monies into our account. When this was done they were to ring me and let me know the total of the money collected. I was absolutely blown away when the bank advised me they had counted $5,324. We were in the clear. It wasn't quite the parting of the Red Sea, but it was no less the work of the Lord.

Coming Full Circle

My experience in Manawahe was made even more special by a significant meeting years before. As you have read, my new life with Jesus began while I was in hospital. Then after three years of change, I made my first visit to a prison. At an AA meeting, a letter was received from Kaitoke Prison requesting members attend an open meeting of AA run by inmates. My sponsor just handed the letter to me and said, 'This is for you Neven.' As it turns out I was one of four who agreed to attend the meeting. The night we went it was very windy and pouring with rain. I could have quite easily stayed at home. But a commitment is a commitment, and we set off for the prison.

When we arrived, I asked myself, "*What am I doing at a place like this?*" I had all sorts of images of what prisoners were like as I had seen films which had portrayed some rough aspects of life behind bars. As we entered the prison and were escorted to the meeting room, the doors were locked behind us, and I started to shake and felt extremely uncomfortable. Were it not for the hand of God, I could have very easily wound up residing in here for a spell.

The members of the prison AA group arrived. Slowly, as the meeting warmed up and we began sharing our common stories, I experienced an incredible sense of calm and peace. Instantly, I knew I was in the place where God wanted me to be, that I would learn about working with those in prison. On the way home that night I said to the others, 'I have to go back and visit the prison again.' Hence, every Monday evening I travelled to Kaitoke Prison to share the hope of recovery from addiction that can be found through the AA programme.

One evening, just as I was preparing for the journey home, a prisoner named Robert came to me and said, 'My higher power, he is someone special.' He then asked if I'd be interested in sharing him with the chapel group on a Wednesday night? I responded with a big yes, as long as he arranged the invitation through the chaplain. The chaplain was happy for me to visit on a Wednesday instead of Monday—I could not afford the time or cost involved in doing both—and it was all approved the next day. So, I started to visit the prison on Wednesday nights to share with the men who wanted to hear the good news about my Lord, my Higher Power, Jesus.

Manawatu Prison Chaplaincy

So my prison work began with a prisoner inviting me to visit and share the good news of salvation found only in Jesus Christ. In a very short time, because of this work, I would meet Charles Colson the author of *Born Again*, and become the chairman of the Manawatu Branch of Prison Fellowship of New Zealand. I would travel to America with Nettie to attend the Presidential Prayer Breakfast hosted by the then-President, Ronald Regan. All this led up to my appointment as Executive Director of Prison Fellowship of New Zealand a position I held until 1989, and then to my appointment as chaplain at Manawatu Prison.

I don't wish to give a detailed account of my experiences working with Prison Fellowship followed by 16 years as chaplain at Manawatu Prison, but I invite you to listen to some of my experiences with an open mind and heart as I witnessed the Word of God come alive in real life situations in prison.

I hope it will reveal how relevant God's Word is for today and how trustworthy He is in every situation. His Word holds the answers to life. Every one of us is unique and special to Jesus. He loves us and wants us to respond to His love in obedience to His teachings and commands. He has a plan for each of us using the gifts and talents we have been given. I have learnt that you can trust His Word in every situation. He is trustworthy and faithful.

I discovered, as I journeyed one day at a time and keeping my focus on Jesus, that I experienced God's miraculous provision for my needs, His equipping and the further development of the skills needed to serve Him.

On one occasion, I was visiting Kaitoke Prison and I asked an inmate, 'You know how much I love my Lord Jesus and you know what

He has done for me over the short time I have truly known Him. How can I share Him more effectively with you and others in prison?'

I thought it was a very good question to ask. In the early days I assumed that everyone needed to be saved. How very arrogant of me. Well this inmate's reply was to send me away heavy-hearted as he challenged me about the reality of my relationship with Jesus. He replied,

> Neven, you are ashamed of Jesus. If Jesus has done what you tell me he has done, you would be asking me the question, 'Do you know Jesus?' You think I will say no and that will be the end. But Neven it's not the end it's the beginning.

What a statement coming from a young man in prison! From that point on, whenever I met a prisoner for the first time, I asked a very simple question: 'What do you believe in? What is so important to you that you would be prepared to die for?' Everyone without exception replied *family*. That answer then allowed me to comment, 'That's exactly what our heavenly Father did for us. He took our punishment upon Himself so that we could receive a royal pardon for our disobedience (sin).'

Later in their sentence, in the course of one of the chapel programmes, I would be able to tell them that life 'sucks', it isn't fair. Bad things happen and sometimes they hit us without warning. I used the example of Nelson Mandela. He spent 25 years in prison for opposing apartheid rule, came out of prison with no bitterness, and became South Africa's president. I also shared from my own experiences. I needed to be rescued from my stupidity; like a drowning man in the sea I had to be saved from my alcoholism, and I was saved by Jesus. I also learnt that while salvation is free and available by faith for everyone, it cost me everything. I had rough and sometimes very difficult situations to face; that's life—God didn't isolate me from them. But He promised to walk with me through those times and comfort me on the way.

I learnt that the emptiness—dis-ease with myself—I experienced in my inner being was my spirit crying out to be connected with God.

Put another way the empty hole in my being is God-shaped, and is only satisfied when I invite Him to take up residence within me.

The experiences and miracles that Jesus performed for me are not unique to me. I realised very early in my Christian journey that Jesus loved me unconditionally, that he took me as I was and made something beautiful out of my self-made nightmare. The Christian song that speaks of my life is 'Something Beautiful' by Bill Gaither.

> Something beautiful, something good
> All my confusion He understood
> All I had to offer Him was brokenness and strife
> But he made something beautiful of my life
>
> If there ever were dreams
> That were lofty and noble
> They were my dreams at the start
> And hope for life's best were the hopes
> That I harbor down deep in my heart
> But my dreams turned to ashes
> And my castles all crumbled, my fortune turned to loss
> So I wrapped it all in the rags of life
> And laid it at the cross

Charles Colson also visited New Zealand in 1984, two years earlier than the visit I have described. On this occasion he spoke at the Wellington Town Hall; the meeting was chaired by the then-mayor of Wellington, Michael Fowler. Colson had been brought to New Zealand by a group of New Zealand businessmen who were in the process of establishing the Prison Fellowship of New Zealand. The businessmen included Keith Hay, Peter Blaxall, Sir Peter Tait, Sir John Marshall, James Worsfold and Barry Botherway. Prison Fellowship was established as a charitable trust in New Zealand in 1983 and Barry Botherway was the first managing director, operating out of Christchurch. Chuck Colson's address that night was powerful and inspirational; I already believed that God was calling me to visit those in prison, so I made the commitment that night to serve the Lord through visiting and supporting people in prison.

The next invitation I received to visit those in prison came from the superintendent of Manawatu Prison. Manawatu Prison had opened as a first-offenders' prison catering for young first offenders. I was asked to share the AA programme with those who might be interested. I arranged to go on a Monday evening for an hour and a classroom in the education block would be open for those wishing to attend.

The first Monday I arrived at the prison I was taken to a classroom and an announcement was made that the AA programme was on for anyone interested. I sat in the classroom for an hour and not one person arrived. I spent that time just reading the Bible and reading AA's *Big Book* as it is affectionally known. It is the story of AA and how it works. At the end of the hour I got up and departed the prison. For four weeks the same procedure took place. I would sit in the classroom for an hour and no one would turn up and I would spend that time reading the Bible and the *Big Book* then leave the prison.

After the four weeks I started to think I was wasting my time and that I could be more effective channelling my time and energies in other directions. So I made the decision I would visit one more time and then advise the superintendent that no one seemed to be interested in meeting. So I went back for one more visit and settled into the classroom expecting no one to turn up. After 10 minutes, to my surprise, two guys walked in and sat down and their first comment to me was, 'You are for real. We have been watching you for the last four weeks and we can see something from your commitment to help us.'

So began a weekly visit to Manawatu Prison under the supervision of the prison chaplain, Graeme Brogden. Graeme became my mentor, someone who taught me how to help and communicate the good news to those in prison.

The important lesson I learnt from this experience was that the good news of Jesus is shared not by words, but through our actions.

I learnt that going and just being there was all that was required. Then watch what God does in drawing people to you out of their curiosity and need.

Years later I was to learn that staff had also been watching me and had been asking themselves, 'What is it about this ex-All Black who comes out to the prison on a voluntary basis to help these guys?'

I wore a lapel pin which read 'Under New Management'. The men in prison asked me what it meant. I would then talk about my experience, that doing things my way and handling my problems on my own had always ended in a real mess. I knew there had to be a better way and selling out to my Lord and placing Him in my life as the decision-maker made real sense. He's the boss and I am his worker, I'm under new management. Jesus the Master Creator looked after me in amazing ways when I called out to Him and did things His way.

> I alone know the plans I have for you, plans to bring you prosperity and not disaster, plans to bring about the future you hope for. Then you will call to me. You will come and pray to me, and I will answer you. You will seek me, and you will find me because you will seek me with all your heart (Jeremiah 29:11–13 GNT).

In 1985 I was asked to consider taking up the position of Executive Director of Prison Fellowship of New Zealand which I had no hesitation in accepting. I travelled all over New Zealand developing a volunteer support network to assist prison chaplains and their work. I also developed 'Project 500' to support the work of Prison Fellowship of New Zealand financially. Project 500 encouraged individuals to pledge a weekly amount paid monthly by an automatic payment through their bank. These contributions were eligible for a tax rebate from Inland Revenue each year.

I received an invitation from Mark Mitchell to speak at a Full Gospel Businessmen's Fellowship meeting in Hamilton and to stay with his family during my visit. Mark and his wife Barbara became my spiritual mentors and advisers. During this visit Mark and Barbara asked me if I had been baptised in the Holy Spirit. I had no idea what they were talking about but they encouraged me to go with them to their upper room and allow them to pray and lay hands on me asking Jesus to baptise me with the Holy Spirit.

While climbing the stairs to the upper room I quietly prayed to Jesus asking him to confirm that if this baptism in the Holy Spirit was for real He would give me a sign. The day was overcast with showers and, as Barbara and Mark started to pray, a bright ray of sunshine burst into the room filling it with warmth and light. It was the sign that I had asked for to confirm that what was happening was from Jesus. Immediately after Mark and Barbara stopped praying the beam of light disappeared; it was overcast again and light rain began to fall.

Being baptised in the Holy Spirit made a major difference to my ministry and relationship with Jesus. When I read the Bible guided by the Spirit it was no longer just a book with a whole lot of stories, it was alive and active and provided revelations of God's big plan for me now and for eternity.

When I was miles away from God doing my thing, my way, I used to think that life was going OK, when in reality the opposite was the case. I was a lonely, insecure and hurting individual completely lost in my own world. In the mess I had created by my own choices and actions, God was waiting for me to respond to His amazing grace, mercy and love. I met the third person of the Trinity that day with Mark and Barbara Mitchell. Everything looked different and I began to see God's word come alive as I ministered to people in need, people God brought across my path that he wanted to minister to through me.

Shortly after taking up the position of Executive Director of the Prison Fellowship of New Zealand, Sir Peter Tait arranged for Jeannette and I to travel to Washington DC to attend the prayer breakfast hosted by the president of the United States. The trip lasted two weeks and we stayed in Los Angeles with friends of Sir Peter Tait. We had no prior idea of where we would be staying in Washington DC, but Sir Peter told us that we would be met at the international airport and taken to our billets. We were taken to meet Sharon and Bill Lett. Bill was secretary of the agriculture department of America and our stay in Washington was a highlight due to their hospitality.

Every day leading up to the prayer breakfast there were seminars hosted by top evangelists from around the world. We went to Prison Fellowship International's seminar led by Chuck Colson; a second seminar we attended was hosted by Louis Palau. Yet another seminar was led by Loren Cunningham, the founder of Youth With a Mission.

Undoubtedly the highlight was the prayer breakfast which is usually held every last Thursday of January and is hosted by the president of the United States. We were addressed by Ronald Reagan and found his address inspiring. He told us the following story which I have related on many occasions.

> In the fourth century in Asia Minor there existed a prayerful monk by the name of Telemachus. His service to the Lord was his prayer ministry. A quiet but diligent man and faithful to his prayer ministry. One day while praying he heard the quiet voice of the Lord say to him, 'Go to Rome.' 'Why me?' he asked. 'I am a nobody and Rome is the centre of the Roman Empire.'
>
> God replied, 'Go to Rome and follow my leading.' Very reluctantly Telemachus journeyed to Rome and continued to pray as led by the spirit.
>
> One day while he was out walking he got caught up in a crowd and he went with them and found himself at the top of the Colosseum. He had no idea at first what was going to take place, but he soon realised the gladiators were going to be fighting to the death. Telemachus jumped to his feet and cried out in a loud voice, 'Stop it in the name of Jesus.' The crowd thinking that this was part of the show clapped and cheered their approval. Telemachus made his way down and into the arena crying out as loud as he could, 'Stop it in the name of Jesus.' The crowd became very hostile towards Telemachus. How dare a monk disrupt their entertainment? The crowd was calling for Telemachus to be put to death. A gladiator

> plunged his sword into the chest of Telemachus and with his last breath he cried out, 'Stop it in the name of Jesus.'
>
> Silence fell on the Colosseum and, one by one, the spectators got to their feet and left. That day was the last time that gladiators fought to the death as entertainment in the Colosseum.

I found out later, that in essence, the story was true but that dates and events vary slightly from the account we heard. Regardless of the minor errors in the story, the point remains. One person who was obedient to the calling of the Lord, sacrificed his life and ended that senseless entertainment.

We attended the official opening of the DeMoss House, a facility that Prison Fellowship USA were going to use as a rehabilitation and discipleship venue. We presented Charles Colson with an unfinished bisque-fired vase with the cross and the Maori symbol of fellowship draped around the cross.

On our return to New Zealand we stopped over in Los Angeles for three days and during that time we visited John MacArthur Jr's church and were very impressed with the hospitality and friendliness of the people in serving the Latin American population, together with the physically handicapped and hearing-impaired members of the congregation. Joni Eareckson Tada was a member of the church who, through a tragic swimming accident, became a paraplegic but who used her faith and musical skills to reach hundreds of thousands with the good news of Jesus Christ.

Entertaining strangers and offering hospitality is a very important part of the lifestyle of a Christian as I found by reading the Bible (Basic Instruction Before Leaving Earth).

> Keep on loving one another as brothers and sisters. Do not forget to show hospitality to strangers, for by so doing some people have shown hospitality to angels without knowing it. Continue to remember those in prison as if you were together with them in prison, and those who are mistreated as if you yourselves were suffering (Hebrews 13:1–3).

This scripture came alive for me in 1987 when I was travelling back from Christchurch to Palmerston North. I had just concluded a tour of the South Island talking to groups of people interested in serving Christ's kingdom through visiting those in prison. I had been to Dunedin, Invercargill and Christchurch and was heading home. It was my birthday. In my quiet time that morning I had again been reading about crime being a spiritual issue. That its solution was to encourage a spiritual awareness in the offender in order to develop his positive character qualities which would always result in their making a contribution to their community, rather than abusing it as they had in the past.

Winston Churchill is reported to have said that if you wanted to know where a country was at spiritually, look at their prison population numbers. They will tell you whether a country is solidly grounded in spiritual values or not. If your prison population is increasing rapidly the spiritual condition of the nation is in decline.

History told me that where there had been a spiritual revival in a nation the immediate evidence of its effect was a decline in criminal offending and a decrease in prison populations. Wales in 1904–5 is the classic example.

As I was travelling back to Palmerston North I made up my mind that I needed a relatively quiet day—a day off—just to relax and catch up from a full-on time of ministry. That meant I would not pick up any hitch-hikers. It was my birthday after all, and a break would be good for me. Well that is what I thought…

God had other plans, of course. As I passed through Kaikoura and approached the city boundary there was a hitch-hiker on the side of the road. I drove on past him but then I was prompted to turn around and go back and pick him up. Very reluctantly I did what I was told to do, turned round, went back and picked up the hitch-hiker. Surprise, surprise… he was going to Picton to catch the ferry to Wellington! The same ferry I was booked on. We chatted about New Zealand and I told him I was going on to Palmerston North and that if he wished to travel with me, there was a bed at our place to rest up if he wanted to. He thanked me for the very generous offer but said he would make Wellington his stopover and catch up with friends. I told him that was fine but if his situation changed the offer was still there.

He then asked me why I turned around and came back to pick him up at Kaikoura. In response I said, 'I'm glad you asked me that question…' and I went on to tell him about my faith in Jesus, how he had met me in my hour of desperate need, and that he had told me by his Spirit to turn around and pick him up. He was very interested in everything I shared with him and we parted our different ways when we arrived at Picton.

Halfway through the passage from Picton to Wellington he found me reading in the forward lounge and asked if he could take up my offer for a ride and a bed in Palmerston North. I said that would be fine and he joined me when it came time to disembark and we travelled home to Palmerston North.

He stayed with us for 10 days and he cooked us a meal that was his favourite back in his homeland. The goulash he prepared for us was fabulous and we enjoyed his company and his stay with us until he departed for Auckland.

It turned out he was struggling with his addiction to drugs; he embraced the message of the gospel and we kept in touch with Christmas greetings and mail about my ministry, right up until I took the chaplaincy position at Manawatu Prison.

We really do not know what God can do through us until we experience his sovereign move to the needy he draws across our paths. That journey was a very special experience and a very unexpected encounter with someone who needed help yet on the surface looked as if he was okay and in control of his life. We can never take the needs of others lightly or for granted.

> This is how you can recognise the Spirit of God: Every spirit that acknowledges that Jesus Christ has come in the flesh is from God,

but every spirit that does not acknowledge Jesus is not from God. This is the spirit of the antichrist, which you have heard is coming and even now is already in the world. You, dear children, are from God and have overcome them, because the one who is in you is greater than the one who is in the world (1 John 4:2–4).

While working with Prison Fellowship I was able to develop a community of voluntary workers, and branches were established in Christchurch, Wellington, Palmerston North and Auckland. I quickly learnt that there were church groups all over New Zealand visiting prisons and supporting the chaplains. Some groups travelled hundreds of miles on a Sunday to visit the prisons at Rangipo, lead services and then travel home. Their commitment to serve the kingdom of God by visiting those in prison was inspiring.

Prison Fellowship of New Zealand supported the establishment of care homes in Auckland, Woodville and Palmerston North for inmates who were released from prison and desired to make a new start living a Christian lifestyle.

These homes were run by individuals operating under established trusts, so Prison Fellowship had no financial obligation for the day-to-day running costs of the homes, only a commitment to support and to assist the right placement of people leaving prison.

Individuals offered to support Jeannette and myself financially in our ministry and so we established a trust to channel that support. Our trust was called Tatau Me Ihu Trust (Together with Jesus) and under that trust we operated a home for young offenders under the age of twenty-one. The property in Ada Street was owned by the All Saints Anglican Family Trust and one of the stipulations in making the facility available, was that it was to be used for young people under the age of twenty-one. Manawatu prison, which was established in 1979, was for first offenders and most of the inmates were under the age of twenty-one. Lattey Lodge, as the house was called, was able to support prisoners being released from Manawatu prison who wanted accommodation and support. The property had a home for the supervisors and four flats, like motel units, that could sleep two people in each unit. We also provided one unit for a live-in mentor that the guys could go to at any time, to receive advice and help with any problem they were experiencing. The mentor also helped with the day-to-day running of the home and modelled a Christian life.

In 1987 I was invited to take up the position of relieving chaplain at Kaitoke Prison. I held this position for six months until a full-time chaplain was appointed. I travelled to Kaitoke Prison, by car each day and occasionally would work 10-hour days due to commitments with programmes. The days when I was not required at Kaitoke Prison I would work on catching up with correspondence and newsletters for Prison Fellowship of New Zealand.

The social worker at Kaitoke Prison was Mrs Salisbury, a committed Christian who was very supportive of my work and involvement at the prison. She gave me great insights about working in the prison environment. On the Wednesday night before Easter in 1987 I had a commitment to speak to a Full Gospel Businessmen's Fellowship meeting in Stratford. After a full day at the prison I travelled in our HiAce van and had a wonderful evening with the members of the fellowship. They pleaded with me to stay the night but I wanted to get home to be with the family for the Easter period. As I approached Wanganui I started to feel very tired and I stopped at the rest area in Kaitoke to stretch my legs and get a bit of fresh air. I really struggled to keep awake on the drive from Kaitoke back to Palmerston North and when I finally reached the city boundary of Palmerston North I said, 'Whew, I'm home' and promptly fell asleep at the wheel. This happened as I was approaching the railway bridge on Rangitikei Street; I just missed the concrete wall at the top of the bridge and plummeted onto the railway line. I came to as the car was falling towards the railway line and everything was happening in slow motion. The front of the van hit the railway lines and then fell onto its roof. I tried to open the driver's door but it wouldn't budge and then I heard a voice telling me to undo my seatbelt and I was helped out of the van. When I got to my feet there was no one in sight. The time was 2 am. I climbed back up the bank to Rangitikei Street and there was no one in sight. I decided to walk up the street to find someone to help me and to notify the police of the accident. As I was approaching Featherston Street a police car with flashing lights passed me heading towards the bridge. So I decided to go back to the scene of the accident where I found the police and railway workers searching for the driver of the van. I went up to the police officer and told him that I was the driver and he immediately enquired if I was all right. I told him that I felt okay but the ambulance had also been called and they decided that I should go to the hospital for a check-up. As a result I was kept in overnight.

I gave the police my home address and phone number, but they decided it would be better to call on Jeannette and tell her about the accident rather than disturbing her by phone. When Jeannette heard the knock on the door she wondered who would be calling at such a late hour. She asked who was there and the police officer replied that he had been talking to her husband, that he had been involved in a car accident and was being held overnight in hospital. The police's approach was greatly appreciated because Jeannette knew immediately that I was all right. When she got to the hospital she found me in good spirits, a little bruised but otherwise okay.

Later that day after I was discharged from hospital, we visited the site of the accident and then went to see the van which was being held at the insurance assessment centre. At the site of the accident you could see quite plainly the van's path from where it left the road to where it ended up on the railway line. But the amazing thing that took our attention was that the glass from the broken windscreen and driver's door was in a neat cone-shaped pile. When we arrived at the insurance assessment centre, the manager stated that he had heard that the driver had walked away relatively unharmed from the van and that had to be a miracle. When we saw the van we understood why he had come to that conclusion, because there was no room for me behind the steering wheel. The whole front of the van had been pushed back and the imprints of the railway lines were obvious.

Mrs Salisbury rang me from Kaitoke prison later that day, asked how I was because at her church prayer meeting on the evening of the accident, she had had a strong sense of calling to pray for me which the whole group supported. When I told her what had happened she just rejoiced and said, 'Praise the Lord.'

In hindsight the accident should never have happened. I should have stayed overnight in Stratford and returned home the following day. But the miraculous outcome of the accident can be put down to the faithful people who prayed, when led by the Spirit to do so. The event gave me a greater understanding that God is always there for me. However, there are events, some very tragic, that I have difficulty accepting. By faith I accept that the sovereign God is in control and that he will help me through the time of trial.

One Door Shuts and Another Opens

In 1989 the board of Prison Fellowship of New Zealand decided that they wanted to move the administration from Palmerston North to Auckland. I informed the board that I had no desire to shift to Auckland. Very reluctantly I tendered my resignation not knowing what work opportunity lay ahead.

I struggled with my employment coming to an end with Prison Fellowship. I had witnessed many miraculous events during my short time as Executive Director. What I discovered later, and it wasn't a long wait, was that God had another opportunity He had prepared for me.

Just after my services with Prison Fellowship ended in 1989 I was encouraged to apply for the position of chaplain at Manawatu Prison. Initially I thought, "What's the use?". New Zealand's Justice Department would not employ people who had a criminal conviction. I needed a lot of persuading and, very reluctantly, I obtained the necessary documents and references and applied for the position, not expecting to be called for an interview.

The time as relieving chaplain at Kaitoke Prison turned out to be the highest recommendation for the position. The then-superintendent, Mr Hines or *Bully* as he was affectionately known, had given me a glowing reference. I found out later that it wasn't my theological qualifications that got me the appointment—because I had none—it was what I had been doing in visiting the prisons and helping where there was a need. My status as an ex-All Black did play a part, as senior staff at the time, were great rugby enthusiasts and I would be an asset to any discussion at morning tea time on that subject. God used every aspect of my past experiences when I made myself available to go where he wanted me to go to minister through me to the lost and confused He wants to reach.

Everything is possible for God. I was appointed chaplain for Manawatu without any qualifications, and with a criminal record. My appointment was the first of many miracles that I witnessed God perform while at Manawatu Prison.

My first day as chaplain was 26 October 1989, on arrival, I reported as requested to Superintendent Lyn Rastrick who gave me a warm welcome and informed me he saw my role as chaplain as being the conscience of the prison. I was to speak up on all issues that violated what I thought was fair treatment of inmates and hold staff accountable for any action that violated the working standards and practices laid down by the Department.

In my role as chaplain I reported directly and solely to the superintendent and it was to him that I was accountable for all my actions within the prison. The Department appointed a senior chaplain and in 1989 that position was held by the Rev Ed Boyd, any matters of chaplaincy welfare were channelled through him to the National Council of Churches, which was responsible to oversee the standard of practice and welfare of prison chaplains. The recommendation by the National Council of Churches to the Justice Department of that time was that there should be one ecumenical chaplain for every 200 inmates. In addition, the Catholic church appointed their own chaplains and their remuneration was paid by the Catholic church.

Three men turned up to my first Sunday chapel service. We sat around and discussed what was important for chapel services to be about for them. The unanimous response was good music and singing, prayer, instruction and practical examples of how to live a Christian life. I knew how important music was, yet I was unable to play any musical instrument and my singing left a lot to be desired. So what do I do? That night while reading God's Scripture a passage just stood out for me. It was:

> I tell you the truth, anyone who has faith in me will do what I have been doing. He will do even greater things than these, because I am going to the Father. And I will do whatever you ask in my name, so that the Son may bring glory to the Father. You may ask me for anything in my name, and I will do it (John 14:12–14 NIV).

Well, I got on my knees and asked God to bring me musicians for the ministry. I was hoping for musicians in the local churches to get together and visit each Sunday and lead worship in the chapel services. God had other plans. Over the next two weeks that prayer was answered. Firstly, a top-line musician who had his own band in Palmerston North, was sentenced for a few years. Then an inmate on transfer from the South Island and heading for Waikeria Prison, found himself placed permanently at Manawatu prison instead. He played lead guitar and was a top musician. In a very short time we had a very good music group including singers. The superintendent gave permission for a local musician to bring his keyboard, mixers and sound equipment into the prison and it was set up in the chapel. The Manawatu prison chapel music group was established and eventually gave themselves the name 'Just Released'. Additional guitars were donated by supportive churches and week by week the music group developed a wonderful repertoire of worship songs as requested by those in the group and the inmates who attended chapel on a regular basis. Added to their repertoire, were songs the group wrote themselves and two years later, they recorded a tape of their music which included songs entitled John 10, Shackles, I Only Wish, Standing Alone, Think Things Over and Be Still just to mention a few and they are available on disc from my website.

The church groups visiting the prison to lead chapel services on a Sunday, were so impressed with the group, they asked me if there was any possibility of taking the group out of prison to visit and lead services in their churches. I approached the superintendent to discuss the idea with him. I added that the prisoners could also share individual testimonies of their changed lives, through encountering Jesus, while participating in the chaplaincy activities and services. His response was very positive and approval was given and arrangements made to take the musical team out to share in church services. These outings occurred on a regular basis and the team was enthusiastically received; they shared their personal stories of life before encountering Jesus, how Jesus found them and what life meant to them now. Their open and honest sharing impacted the congregations and gave hope that there truly was a positive way to deal with crime and reduce reoffending.

I received many requests from churches in the Manawatu region to share my vision of the ministry at Manawatu Prison. I would tell the people a little of my journey of faith with Jesus and then tell them what God was doing at the prison and how he had established a very competent and professional music and choir group, which called themselves 'Just Released'. The result of these church visits resulted in churches wanting to be involved with the prison ministry. Over a relatively short period I had 10 church groups wanting to visit the prison on a Sunday to lead chapel services and I developed a really professional volunteer group that supported the chaplaincy and the programmes that were established over the first two years.

The next significant event occurred when I was approached by an inmate, asking me what programmes I could provide that would help him make positive changes to his lifestyle. He had attended various courses over a number of years and nothing seemed to work for him. At that time, we had some very qualified professionals, sentenced for a wide range of offences. I obtained permission to have a group of eight inmates in the chapel, for a whole day to brainstorm ideas for a programme that would address the issues they were concerned about. That day was truly inspirational for me, as I watched these men explore topics they wanted to find out more about to make alterations to their thinking, attitudes and behaviour.

At the end of the day the group had come up with the following topics:

- Identity (Who Am I?)
- Feelings/emotions
- Relationships
- Communication
- Addictions
- Self-esteem
- Anger
- Goals/objectives
- Self-acceptance/awareness
- Hurts and guilt

I recommended that the programme should be facilitated by those doing the programme working in pairs and they should research the topic assigned to them. They would be allowed to present their module any way they wanted to. I agreed to prepare some guidelines for the facilitators.

The programme was called at this stage HELP or the 'High Energy Life Programme' but was later changed to the PVA Programme or 'Principles, Values and Attitudes'. I developed 12 traditions and steps for it, based on the Alcohol Anonymous programme of recovery.

These are the qualities I suggested a good facilitator should have. A facilitator must be able to:

- Learn from experience
- Accept others
- Listen well
- Be optimistic
- Be cheerful
- Be non-judgemental
- Keep a confidence
- Encourage decision-making
- Be supportive
- Be patient
- Control their own feelings

When facilitating a module, it was recommended that the group should sit in a circle so all members were involved, and have the group acknowledge the programme protocols, as follows:

- Anything shared in the programme was confidential and remained in the group
- Only one person could speak at a time
- Listen to what is shared
- Members need to make a personal commitment to complete the programme so there is no quitting or walking out of the course
- Members need to put aside their prejudices and personality clashes while attending the programme
- When sharing, each member of the group had to own their comments by using 'I'. Further, when feelings, thoughts, beliefs and opinions were shared they weren't up for debate or discussion

- For the introductory first session the suggested format was, 'Hi. My name is John and I want to share with you why I'm attending this programme, how I feel right now, what my interests are, how I spend my time, and the people who are important to me and how I have affected them by coming to prison.'

The programme was structured to run one module a week for two hours over a 12-week period. The first week was spent setting up the protocols for the group and the participants introducing themselves, while certificates were presented and the programme evaluated in the last week.

Several inmates, when they had completed the programme, asked if they could do it again as they had learnt so much about themselves and the topics discussed. They found the programme very helpful; the group members were very supportive and they had learnt about themselves by listening to others with similar issues.

It was important that the programme was flexible in order to meet the specific needs of the group whether gender or cultural. The most important factor for the participants to remember was that while the PVA programme gave them knowledge and skills, for change and growth to occur, they had to *apply* the principles, values and attitudes they had learnt; in their everyday living and learn to make the right choices. They needed to practice new thinking processes to develop the right attitudes and behaviour while in the prison environment and then continue the process when released back into the community.

The proverb that became the motto for the programme was 'I hear–I forget; I see–I know; I do–I understand. The PVA programme was successful because the inmates took ownership of it and made it work. We learnt that the simple equation 'our attitude + our choices = our life' was the key to the programme.

In 1996 I was introduced to the Church Army, a branch of the Anglican Church. They had a yacht, the *Sarah Jane*, which could be charted for discipleship programmes. I made enquiries about taking nine inmates from Manawatu prison on a discipleship course. This involved learning about navigation, sailing and living a life of discipline following the example of Jesus Christ. The cost of a nine-day discipleship course was $350 per person which included all meals. Ian Moody, a youth minister with the Anglican church, would be leading the instruction in the discipleship programme, and the owner of the vessel would teach sailing skills; as well as the information required to pass the test on navigation at the end of the course.

I approached Henny Ledivelt, who was prison superintendent at that time, and he gave approval for the trip to take place under my supervision; as long as no costs associated with the trip were debited to the prison or the Department. Each inmate was sponsored by a church and that support came from as far away as Hamilton.

Nine inmates were released into my care for nine days while we travelled to Auckland, where the discipleship programme was being held on board the *Sarah Jane*. We lived in very cramped conditions aboard the *Sarah Jane*. For all of us, it was an amazing encounter with the reality of faith in Jesus Christ and God's wonderful provision for his people who reach out for his help. The whole trip passed without incident.

The prison provided one of their 12-seater vans and I was to drive the van at all times; the petrol costs would come out of funds raised. On the first day we travelled to Totara Springs Christian Centre, just out of Matamata, in the Waikato and the following day travelled on to Auckland and boarded the *Sarah Jane*. The first night was anything but smooth sailing, with me spending most of the night feeding the fish! I'm not a good sailor at any time. I was very seasick indeed. The skipper took pity on me and sheltered in the bay off Tiritiri Matangi Island. The next day we proceeded to Kawau Island and moored in Bon Accord Harbour where we were going to stay for the next three days.

Each day would start with a time of worship, prayer and Bible study followed by breakfast. The rest of the day would be spent studying sailing, navigation, and taking scenic walks on the island. In the evening after tea, there would be another time of worship and Bible study followed by discipleship instruction. After the first three days we would apply what we had learnt in navigation and sailing by taking day trips from Kawau Island. On the second to last day of the course, each member was tested on navigation and sailing skills and everyone passed and received a certificate to mark their achievement.

On arrival back in Auckland we spent one night with the brothers of St Francis of Assisi and the group was informed of the work undertaken by the brothers, led by Brother Paul. Everyone in our group was impressed by the brothers' commitment to their faith and their service to the communities where they were placed.

The next day we travelled to Hamilton and were hosted by the Friday Fellowship, a group of ladies from all churches called to minister to the needy in Hamilton. Again our group got an insight into what life was like serving the needs of others. In a time of quiet reflection the ladies ministered to our group, individually, praying for needs and issues which needed to be addressed. That time was very special and tears were shed and past hurts, guilt and shame were released in prayer and given to God.

Years later, reflecting on that trip, I realised that only one of the nine men who participated, returned to prison for reoffending. In fact, it wasn't so much reoffending as it was clearing away past offences that he confessed to the authorities. For me personally, the trip was very hard and living conditions very cramped, but the result made all that hardship worthwhile. Information about the trip was released to the media by a disgruntled prison officer and it hit the billboards: 'Prisoners go cruising on the Hauraki Gulf.' The article was very biased and negative about the trip, but presented no facts about the trip and its objectives were never mentioned, which was very disappointing.

When I was working for Prison Fellowship, I obtained study material produced by Bill Gothard through the Christian Life Centre Bookshop. Arnold and Janet Kimberly, who owned the shop imported this material from America. I learnt with interest, about the programmes Gothard had developed, especially the Basic Life Skills programme, and was delighted to learn that he was to visit Palmerston North and run the programme here. I again jumped at the opportunity and asked if I could take inmates to the event, which was being run over a few evenings. Permission was granted and Meterina Savage and I took two inmates to the seminar. I was very impressed with the content of the programme, as it gave the basic steps to deal with life issues, which we meet and need to handle on a daily basis. This programme complimented the PVA programme, which had already been established and I negotiated for the Basic Life Principles seminar to be held in the prison. We ran the programme on three occasions and it was well attended and very beneficial for those desiring to make changes to their lifestyle and the participants recognised they had made some very bad choices.

When I used to visit the prison to support Graeme Brogden, he ran an informal Thursday night meeting, where he would show a film followed by a discussion. The films always had a Christian message covering testimonies, feature films and documentaries. The discussions were inspiring as individuals shared which different aspects of the evening's film, had impressed them and related to their own experiences. The evening always concluded with one of the visitors summing up the film and relating it to Scripture. This process had always impressed me, as it showed that God's word was not just stories but had a practical application to living our life today.

Over time, I developed other programmes which worked in a practical sense, so that inmates were confronted with dealing with their own issues and not just putting them aside or sweeping them under the carpet. The most suitable material by far was Bill Gothard's Basic Life Principles and all his Institute's associated videos and published material. It gave individuals a sound basis for their faith. But I hastened to assure the inmates that knowing the basis of the Christian way of life, must never be based on a manual. I would stress, that faith involved walking with the Lord and being led and taught by

Him, through the Holy Spirit. Faith, was doing everything God's way, not our way.

New technology saw the development from film projection, to video players and finally DVD players and the development of Christian films. Dramatised Bible stories and testimonies, greatly enhanced the positive aspects of faith and created an attitude of *hope* in the lives of inmates, who desperately sought change. Bill Gothard's 'Chalk Talk', highlighting character qualities was inspirational. Rob Harley's 'Journeys', a five-week odyssey, examining the Christian faith through real people, was another programme which created a real positive foundation for change.

We were very fortunate with the support teams from the churches in Palmerston North and they formed a roster to lead the chapel services. We went from one chapel a day, to holding three every Sunday: one in the morning for remand and high security inmates, one in the afternoon for segregated inmates, and one in the evening for medium and low-security inmates. I always told the church leaders that when selecting their members, to make sure Jesus was real and alive in their witness, because I had found in visiting prisons around New Zealand and in Australia; that inmates could identify the reality of Jesus in people and those who were not the real deal! They could discern a phony, a mile away.

In addition to the church groups we had individuals visiting on Monday nights and Thursday nights to support Bible studies and our film evenings. These people were committed to serving those in prisons and their contribution was immense. I was always looking for testimonies of people who had a story to tell about what a difference Jesus had made to their lives and we had visitors from all over New Zealand and from overseas. For example, some of our visitors included:

- Bill Subritzky, who had a powerful prophetic ministry.
- The Evangelical Sisters of Mary (Protestant) are an international and interdenominational Christian community.

Their Australian centre, established in 1981, is called 'Canaan of God's Comfort'. It is the base for their ministry throughout Australia, New Zealand, South East Asia, the Pacific Islands and the Indian subcontinent. They are actively involved in the local community and are also invited to hold retreats and to speak at churches and groups in the local area and across Australia. Their ministry being very sensitive and caring and they radiated the presence of the Lord.

- Angus Buchan, an evangelist from South Africa, spent a whole day with us at the prison; and his dynamic prophetic ministry was powerful and effective.
- Stephen Lungu, also from Africa and author of *Out of the Black Shadows*, shared his testimony of his journey from the demonic and gang scene to his role as evangelist for the Christian faith
- The 'Shekinah Glory Music Team' from New Plymouth led by Kobi Hart, visited the prison on many occasions sharing in worship, testimonies, God's word and ministering to individual needs as highlighted in Kobi's prophetic utterances. The Shekinah Glory music and worship sessions were of a high professional standard and loved by all who attended.

All this professional input into the chaplaincy ministry at Manawatu Prison led to the establishment of the Christian unit, Alpha, in April 2000. While there was some scepticism when it was first established, it proved to have positive benefits for the staff and for the inmates who were placed in the unit. The number of incident reports from Alpha were substantially less than other units. In the first five years, very few incident reports needed to be processed and, if my memory is correct, there were only eight.

If an inmate wanted to be considered for the Alpha unit they had to make an application in writing; they were also required to sign the Code of Conduct for the unit. This was the first-ever and only Christian unit established in a New Zealand Prison and the Operating Principles Manual, which was developed for the unit, provided a guideline for other units that might be established in the future.

I will always be convinced that the only way that we can reduce crime in New Zealand is through the criminal experiencing a radical change of mind and heart by a spiritual awakening. Two publications, the Roper Report in 1989 and Samuel Yochelson and Stanton Samenow in their book *The Criminal Personality – A Profile for Change (1971)*, agreed that the conventional methods of dealing with crime then, were not working. After years of research Yochelson and Samenow stated that conventional housing of criminals wasn't working and what was needed was for the criminal to have a conversion experience.

The other really positive ceremony I performed at Manawatu Prison was baptism. The baptismal services were very special events and each one was uniquely different. The highest number of baptisms in one night was eight. One thing I learnt with these services was that you could never tell how long a baptism would take, as God met people at their point of need. The Holy Spirit moved sovereignly, when invited, at these services. Initially, I would do what occurs at a church full immersion baptism, assisting the person being baptised going down into the water and then assisting them up onto their feet. On one occasion when I asked the usual questions—'Do you believe that Jesus Christ is the son of God, that he was born of the Virgin Mary, that he suffered under Pontius Pilate, died and was buried, but rose again, ascended into heaven and will come back to judge the living and the dead'—the answers were all yes, so I prayed, 'Holy Spirit come,' and before I could do anything the inmate had disappeared under the water. I hurriedly went to his aid to get him onto his feet. Just as I was getting him to his feet he disappeared again under the water and eventually a chair was needed for him to sit on while God ministered to his needs. That baptism taught me, that God wanted to meet individuals in a special way and it was better for me to keep out of the process. At the next baptism, I again asked the formal questions, which are the basis of the Christian faith. I then asked for Holy Spirit to come and minister to the needs of the individual and that we would wait upon him. I would say, 'Come Holy Spirit, have your way.' The inmate had his hands crossed across his chest and, with eyes closed, waited on the Holy Spirit and, without any assistance from me, would go under the water and be raised in the power of the risen Christ. Inevitably prayers were offered and individuals would give a word from Scripture for the inmate who had just been baptised.

If I had any doubt about the relevance of adult baptism, the experiences I witnessed in the prison emphasised the importance of adult baptism. The prison ministry was really fortunate to have access to St Albans' portable baptismal pool and I would go into town with a prison van, pick the pool up from the church, take it into the chapel and assemble it ready for the service, then return it to the church after we had had the service, usually the following day.

When baptismal services were being held non-believing inmates wanted to be present to see what happened. They were particularly intrigued by what happened in the pool and wanted to find out what I did to the inmate being baptised to make him go under the water. Curiosity about our sovereign God, always has a major impact on those seeking answers to their own life. I always encouraged visitors to come right up to the pool and watch events as they unfolded. The inmates who hadn't encountered Jesus, would be fascinated that I did nothing in the process of the immersion of the inmate into the water and questions would fly: How? Why? What's happening? The events were always well attended and a great witness to the non-believers.

The last, and I guess the most important, question the prisoners asked me about, was heaven and hell and they wanted answers they could relate to. Jesus talked a lot about both places. So I related the question about heaven to a destination. I would tell the prisoners that I can't travel anywhere in the world and enter another nation or kingdom without proof of my identity and approval to enter. I need my passport and visa. Without them I would be refused entry. I would then read the truth from God's Word. It is recorded that Jesus, when talking to a very knowledgeable and learned man, told him:

> 'I am telling you the truth: no one can see the Kingdom of God without being born again.'
>
> 'How can a grown man be born again?' Nicodemus asked. 'He certainly cannot enter his mother's womb and be born a second time!'
>
> 'I am telling you the truth,' replied Jesus, 'that no one can enter the Kingdom of God without being born of water and the Spirit' (John 3:3–5 GNT).

Then Jesus tells him how to be saved from breaking God's order and laws for life and how to become a citizen of the kingdom of God. Jesus told Nicodemus:

> For God loved the world so much that he gave his only Son, so that everyone who believes in him may not die but have eternal life. For God did not send his Son into the world to be its judge, but to be its saviour (John 3:16–17 GNT).

I would then say that being born again of water and the spirit is like getting your passport and visa to enter the kingdom of God. I would ask if that made sense of their question and back came their answer: 'Yes, but what about hell?'

I would reply, 'It's a place without God and without love.'

I would again go back to God's Word and read to them from John 10:9–11 (GNT):

> Jesus said, 'I am the gate. Those who come in by me will be saved; they will come in and go out and find pasture. The thief comes only in order to steal, kill, and destroy. I have come in order that you might have life—life in all its fullness. I am the good shepherd, who is willing to die for the sheep.'

My final comment to them was that when they travel overseas, they will make a choice where they want to go and have the appropriate documentation. Ponder this question: When your life ends and you begin the final journey, what is your destination? It's your choice.

Initially I struggled with all the issues about faith. The Bible made very little sense to me and I can understand people saying it is a collection of myths and tales. For me, the Bible came alive only when I met the author.

> It is God himself who makes us, together with you, sure of our life in union with Christ; it is God himself who has set us apart, who has placed his mark of ownership upon us, and who has given us the Holy Spirit in our hearts as the guarantee of all that he has in store for us (2 Corinthians 1:21–22 GNT).
>
> And you also became God's people when you heard the true message, the Good News that brought you salvation. You believed in Christ, and God put his stamp of ownership on you by giving you the Holy Spirit he had promised (Ephesians 1:13 GNT).

When I walked by faith, God Himself communicated to me by the Holy Spirit. My obedience to Jesus my Lord and Saviour was all important for me.

My journey started by hearing God's Word, responding to his love and promises, and knowing deep within myself that I need to change, to know peace and to be free from guilt and shame. Jesus found me in a real mess, but He made something beautiful out of my life.

Conclusion

Thank you for journeying through my story with me. The parable of the Prodigal Son from Luke 15:17–20 relates to my life in many ways, and you would've noted how Joe Rooney skilfully weaved this into his poem about the jersey. I won't retell the story of the Prodigal Son, but I encourage those of you who haven't read it to do so and hopefully draw inspiration from it.

As this project has grown so have I. Initially, I wanted something my family, friends and historians could read and research. However, I started to realise my true calling for this book, was to help you, as other authors have helped me.

I have journeyed from a place of dishonesty, desolation and despair and found the truth and reality about myself. In the process I found honesty, happiness and joy. It would make me feel even better if you, the reader, take from this story some inspiration. No matter what situation you might face in life, there is hope. Strangely, the answer is not out there with any organisation, government or people. It lies deep within ourselves, we have the *power* and potential to create or destroy. We must be accountable for the choices we make and take responsibility for the outcomes, both good and bad. Thus, true power is the chance to recreate goodness, peace, and harmony for ourselves and those around us.

Appendix A

Curriculum Vitae for IN MacEwan

IN MacEwan (known as Neven, but by most people known as just plain Nev). My background and achievements are:

Experience & Achievements

1951–1952	First fifteen, Nelson College, Nelson, NZ
1952	Lady Godley Shooting Trophy, Nelson College, Nelson, NZ
1952	Sixth Form Certificate, Nelson College, Nelson, NZ
1953–1954	C Certificate, Teachers College, Wellington, NZ
1953	Teachers College Rugby Representative, Wellington, NZ
1953	Wellington RFU Junior Representative, Wellington, NZ
1954–1966	Senior Team, Athletic RFC, Wellington, NZ
1954–1966	Wellington RFU Representative, Wellington, NZ (134 Matches)
1955	All Black Reserve
1956–1962	All Black (55 Matches)
1958–1968	Freight, Travel and Public Relations Officer for Shaw Savill & Albion Co Ltd
1963–1964	Captain, Blackheath RFC, London, UK
1964	Barbarians Representative, London, UK

NEVEN MACEWAN

EXPERIENCE & ACHIEVEMENTS (CONT.)

1964–1966	Captain, Coach and Player of Athletic RFC
1965	Athletic RFC won Premier Championship (Jubilee Cup)
1966	Organised and captained Athletic RFC World Tour to England, Ireland, Hong Kong and Japan
1968–1971	Co-founded, and worked for, the travel company MacEwan-Williment World Travel, Wellington, NZ
1972–1979	Public Relations Officer for the city of Palmerston North, NZ
1973–1974	Coordinated fundraising activities for Palmerston North's contribution to the 1974 Commonwealth Games
1973–1975	Chairman Queen Elizabeth College RFC, Palmerston North, NZ
1973–1975	Senior Rugby Coach Queen Elizabeth College RFC, Palmerston North, NZ
1975	Developed the concept of Palmerston North being a conference venue for New Zealand and founded the Convention Centre Bureau
1976	Organised the Australian tour and sponsorship for Queen Elizabeth College RFC, Palmerston North, NZ
1975–1976	Organised the Ranfurly Shield parades for the city of Palmerston North, NZ
1976–1979	Elected City Councillor for Palmerston North and Chairman of the Economic Development Committee
1976–1979	Chairman of the Rugby Museum Society of New Zealand
1977	Organised the Palmerston North City 'Rose Sunday' promotion in conjunction with TV3
1978	Organised the opening of the Rugby Museum by the Governor General of New Zealand in its first official home
1978	Coordinated the live television broadcast of the Miss New Zealand Contest in Palmerston North, NZ
1979–1985	Massey University Laboratory Technician in the Large Animal Hospital of the Veterinary Science Faculty, Palmerston North, NZ

APPENDIX A

1986–1989	Executive Director, Prison Fellowship of New Zealand, Palmerston North, NZ:

- Developed a volunteer support network throughout New Zealand to support the prison chaplaincy work
- Established financial support from the church community for the ministry of Prison Fellowship from its infancy in New Zealand in 1986 through 'Project 500'

1989–2005	Prison Chaplain, Manawatu Prison, Linton, NZ

- Responsible for organising a group of 260 volunteers to encourage people in prison to adopt the principles and values of Jesus Christ for life

1991	Ordained a Vocational Deacon of the Anglican Church of Aotearoa
1999	Named one of the Legends of Wellington RFU Team of the Century
1959–Now	The raising of our family of four achievers and what they are accomplishing today. Our ten grandchildren and great-grandchild are a real blessing and a credit to their parents.

Personal Statement

I believe in the value of the individual and the potential each has. My chosen vocation for the last 30 years has been to encourage others to maximise that potential by focussing on the gifts and talents that truly satisfy their efforts and achievements.

We live in a multicultural society and it is important to embrace the qualities and the richness of each culture to encourage our future heritage as a nation.

My spiritual journey has been a growing awareness of the continual change required as I build my new life in Christ—the culture of the kingdom of God, as Jesus Christ teaches me through His commands.

My calling is to continue to be in the type of role that enables me to combine these beliefs.

NEVEN MACEWAN

Appendix B

1. More About Joe Rooney

> Dad hasn't been too well so apologies for being a bit late getting this to you Neven. We've had him here with us for a few weeks; he returns to Waikanae on Thursday. He's fine but he tires frequently nowadays. I had him checked out at my quacks and he's doing okay and we've given him a few weeks of R&R and fed him up as much as we can.
>
> Take care.
>
> Just to explain… Dad was only 15 when he joined the navy after forging a letter of permission from 'his mother'. His spelling was so bad that he told the recruitment officer his mum was foreign and couldn't speak much English.
>
> From Joe and his secretary Jeannie

I, Joe Rooney, was born in the Rhondda Valley at 40 Wengraig Road, Trealew during the General Strike of 1926. I remember the Great Depression and all its misery, when the miners and their families suffered appalling conditions. Hunger was a way of life; no wonder the so-called ruling class were so despised by the Welsh.

War broke out in 1939 and the whole world changed. I joined the Air Force cadets but, being too young for the services, I signed on the pool for the Merchant Navy in 1941. I saw service in the North and South Atlantic, Caribbean, Gulf of Mexico, Indian Ocean and the Red Sea. Home on leave in 1943 I met my future wife, Valmae, shortly after I had a medical discharge owing to an injury sustained at sea. Val and I worked as lathe operators in the same factory and I joined the 25th Glamorganshire Regiment of the Home Guard. My main duty in the Home Guard was as a guard at the South Wales Power Plant.

Val and I married on 13 March 1945 in the Catholic church at Tonypandy. Our son, Michael, was born in June 1946 in Llwynypia; our son Kieron was born in the same house as myself in 1948. I changed my job as an assistant safety mines inspector, in charge of the Bevin Boys at Llwynypia Colliery, and went back to work in the Pandy Pits, Penygraig. I didn't like being an official so I left and worked as a collier at Trehafod Colliery.

But I didn't want any child of mine to go into the mines and therefore left and travelled to England for a better life and worked for Metropolitan-Vickers in Manchester in 1948, where my daughter was born in 1950 at Gorse Hill, Stretford in Manchester (She's very quick to tell you that she was conceived in Wales—'I am not a Pom!'). I was employed by Metropolitan-Vickers as a fitter/core builder and was sent out to New Zealand in 1957 to do repair work on the generators at the Whakamaru Power Station, Mangakino and the Islington Substation in Christchurch.

The weather, lifestyle and extremely healthy-looking children convinced me that this was the place I needed to be and I began planning my return to New Zealand and to bring my family with me.

On my return to Manchester, I originally began enquiries to emigrate but had to shelve that as we had more than the number of children permitted. So I quit my job, sold my home, raised the necessary fares and we set sail for New Zealand, not as immigrants, but as full fare-paying passengers. We cannot be called ten-pound poms! That was in 1959. We sailed on the MS Rangitoto at a total cost of five hundred pounds. It doesn't sound much now but when we arrived in

New Zealand almost six weeks later, there was very little left in the bank; the 'bank' being a sock in the drawer.

Thanks to the Cooper family—Curly, Marge, Gary and Rosalie—who assisted with accommodation by providing a caravan and bach, we survived the first year and we are eternally grateful for their help and friendship.

I was employed by the Ministry of Works on various power stations before being transferred from Aratiatia to Turangi, where I spent the better part of 39 years. Rugby played a huge part in my life in Aratiatia and Turangi. I was one of five foundation members of the Pihanga Rugby Club in 1966, president for fourteen years, over two terms; King Country delegate, Sub-Union delegate (where I served as chairman), and president and member of various subcommittees for a period of over thirty years. I first met Nev McEwan in the late 60s along with the late Mick Williment. I was invited by College Old Boys RFC, Palmerston North, to attend an end of year function, along with the late Jim Heaphy, the late John (Flea) Fleury and his brother Bill, and Alan New. Neven was MC for the night, and we were all invited back to Nev's home afterwards, where we met his lovely wife Jeannette.

And so began the tale of that special jersey.

2. Correspondence

Nigel, to you and Dudley and all members of the club,

A big thank you for a memorable night which we still talk about and will continue to talk about in the years ahead. Thank you for your generosity in releasing my jersey to come home for the family. Now I know how much it means to Angus and the family as a whole. Our time with you all was very special but so very short. There was a spirit within the club which to us was encouraging and special. So please convey to all our very heart-warm thanks and appreciation for a superb evening.

Could I ask you to supply the names of those who made presentations to me that night? Their names and the organisations they represented; it will help us to correctly acknowledge all those involved. We again wish the club continued success in providing and nurturing rugby at the most important level and roots of the game.

Sorry we had to beat you so soundly on the Saturday following, but this side of ours is very good, something quite unique.

Blessings to all,
Neven and Angus MacEwan

—·—

Dear Neven and Angus,

Hope you arrived safely home. Yes the function was good to say the least and everyone who attended will remember the night for a very long time. I hope your visit to Ireland went well and you enjoyed the craic as they say.

I believe you really enjoyed yourself at the club which will always have a place for the MacEwan family. The two shirts you presented to the club are awesome. If in fifty years should Joe Rokococo want his shirt returned, as with yourself, he will be more than welcome at the club.

As for the presentations you so rightly received:

The Pontypridd school's tie and book were presented by Mr Gerwyn Caffery, an ex-player of the club who teaches at the local Welsh orientated school and is secretary of the school's rugby.

The wooden rugby ball was presented by Dudley Lloyd, our chairman on behalf of the club.

Club ties, by the president Graham Hill to you and to Angus.

APPENDIX B

The plaque of the Wales Grand Slam was from the club, but presented by ex-Wales, British Lions and Llanelli player, Tommy David.

I presented Angus with a personal gift of a club jersey and club memento which I hope he will treasure, as I will treasure the tie and pin/badge I received from yourself.

The Welsh Grand Slam shirt was presented by Mr Ray Wilton who is a Welsh Rugby Union representative for our district, also the small Welsh whisky and a district tie.

Lastly your wonderful All Black shirt was returned to its rightful owner by the son of Mr Cyril Mahoney, known as Syd, who is an ex-captain of our club.

If possible, could you send a copy of the local paper if it includes details of your visit? The photographer took some good photos so if you could forward a few for us to put with our new jerseys in pride of place, back in the cabinet, that would be great. There is a big hole there now where your shirt used to be. As for the games, well what a team. Of course if Graham Henry and Steve Hansen had not learnt so much when they coached Wales they would not be the force they are today. As I told Angus in an email before the games your third team could probably beat anyone up here in the Northern Hemisphere.

We received a letter from Roddy Evans thanking us for the invitation. He and his son had a great time and he told us he met up with you on the Sunday at Porthcawl.

Well I will close now; I've babbled on enough. I still get a good feeling when I think of the night. It was a great pleasure to meet you and Angus. Please stay well and give my best wishes to Angus and your family.

You will always have good friends at Cilfynydd Rugby—that's KILL-VUN-ITH Rugby.

Best regards,
Nigel E Jones

NEVEN MACEWAN

Appendix C

Match Details

1. New Zealand All Blacks versus British Lions

Date	29 August 1959
Location	Lancaster Park, Christchurch
Final score	22–8 to New Zealand
Referee	C R Gillies
Scorers	**NZ:** Tries – Caulton (2), Meads, Urbahn; DB Clarke – 2 conversions, penalty and drop goal.
	Lions: Tries – Hewitt; Faull – a conversion and penalty
Teams	**NZ:** DB Clarke (Waikato), RH Brown (Taranaki), TR Lineen (Auckland), RW Caulton (Wellington), JF McCullough (Taranaki), RJ Urbahn (Taranaki), MW Irwin (Otago), RC Hemi (Waikato), WJ Whineray (Canterbury) Captain, SF Hill (Canterbury), IN MacEwan (Wellington), KR Tremain (Canterbury), RJ Conway (Otago), CE Meads (Kings Country)

British Lions: KJF Scotland, PB Jackson, MJ Price, D Hewitt, AJF O'Reilley, JP Horrocks-Taylor, REG Jeeps, HF McLeod, AR Dawson Captain, BGM Wood, WR Evans, RH Williams, HJ Morgan, J Faull, GK Smith.

2. New Zealand All Blacks versus Northern Transvaal

Date	19 June 1960
Location	Pretoria
Final score	27–3 to New Zealand
Referee	HPA Hofmeyer
Scorers	**NZ:** Tries – Peter Jones (2), T. Lineen. D Clarke – 3 conversions, 3 penalties
	Northern Transvaal: Holton – 1 penalty
Teams	**NZ:** DB Clarke, McMullen, Laidlaw, Watt; Lineen, AH Clarke, Briscoe, Conway, Gillespie, Meads, MacEwan, Jones, Irwin, Young, IJ Clarke.
	Northern Transvaal: D Holton, L Fourie, F van Rensburg, J Pieterse, R Twigge, G Antelme, E Bourquin, J Myburgh, FJ de Klerk, W Matthyser (captain), J van der Merwe, W Vermaas; HJ Bekker, D van der Heever, JL Myburgh.

APPENDIX C

3. New Zealand versus Eastern Province

Date	13 July 1960
Location	Port Elizabeth
Final score	16–3 to New Zealand
Referee	KRV Carlson
Scorers	**NZ:** Tries – Pickering, Conway, Truter. D Clarke – 2 conversions, 1 penalty.
	NT: Wentzel – penalty.
Teams	**NZ:** DB Clarke, Caulton, Laidlaw, McMullen, Lineen, AH Clarke, Urbahn, Conway, Pickering, Horsley, MacEwan (captain), Gillespie, IJ Clarke, Boon, Anderson.
	Eastern Province: CA Ulyate, H Truter, GJ Oberholster, BR van Deventer, JM Walker, GJ Wentzel, JN Singleton, RD Johnson, T Schonken, PB Allen (captain), RN Griesel, EK Moorcroft, WH Parker, FO Hansen, DN Holton.

4. New Zealand All Blacks versus South Africa —Fourth Test

Date	27 August 1960
Location	Port Elizabeth
Final score	8–3 to South Africa
Referee	RD Burmeister
Scorers	**NZ:** D Clarke – penalty
	SA: Tries – Pelser. Lockyear – 1 penalty, 1 conversion
Teams	**NZ:** DB Clarke, RW Caulton, RF McMullen, KF Laidlaw, JR Watt; WA Davies, KC Briscoe, WJ Whineray (captain), D Young, IJ Clarke, KR Tremain, IN MacEwan, RH Horsley, CE Meads, RJ Conway.
	SA: LG Wilson, HJ van Zyl, IA Kirkpatrick, JL Gainsford, MJ Antelme, K Oxlee, RJ. Lockyear, SP Kuhn, GF Malan, PS du Toit, GH van Zyl, AS Malan (captain), HF van der Merwe, HJM Pelser, DJ Hopwood.

Acknowledgements

I wish to publicly acknowledge the following people for their important role in assisting in my recovery from alcoholism, encouraging my new life in Christ Jesus, and helping me to put this story together. In addition, I want to thank the people who helped me in the prison ministry from 1989–2005 at Manawatu Prison.

Jeannette

Douglas, Bruce, Angus, Jeannie and their families

Ken Edgecombe, Kevin Vincent and Seamus Coogan

Robyn Appleby, Tony Fayerman, Jeannette MacEwan and Helen Moulder

The Right Reverend David (deceased) and Jean Penman

Pastor John and Yvonne Walton

Mark and Barbara (deceased) Mitchell

Bob and Margot Greenway

Arnold (deceased) and Janet Kimberley (deceased)

Bill and Felicity Kimberley

Kevin (deceased) and Eunice O'Sullivan (deceased)

Robyn Booker (née) O'Sullivan

John Loveday

John and Jenny Hornblow

Acknowledgements (cont'd)

Joy Senior

Warren and Prue Sisarich

Bruce Gordon and his mother Reene

George (deceased) and Beryl Rose

Barry (deceased) and Linda Thompson

Canon Doug (deceased) and Jane Edmiston (deceased)

Mr. Gary Rohloff, formerly managing director of Ezibuy Ltd

Robin and Andrea McKenzie

Monsignor Tom Duffy (deceased)

The Right Reverend Brian and Mae Carrell

The Right Reverend Dr Peter Carrell, Bishop of Christchurch

Reverend Michael Godfrey

Anne Penman

Pastor Rodney Francis

Reverend John Niven

Rae Bell (deceased)

Bully Hines

Sir Peter Tait (deceased)

Reverend Paul Dwyer

Sisters of Mary, North Sydney, Australia

The management and staff at Manawatu Prison

All members of Alcoholics Anonymous

The Body of Christ in Palmerston North and throughout New Zealand

www.ingramcontent.com/pod-product-compliance
Lightning Source LLC
Chambersburg PA
CBHW051357290426
44108CB00015B/2052